WHAT IS ECONOMICS?

THIRD EDITION

WHAT IS ECONOMICS?

THIRD EDITION

James Eggert
University of Wisconsin, Stout

Bristlecone Books

Mayfield Publishing Company
Mountain View, California
London • Toronto

Library of Congress Cataloging-in-Publication Data
Eggert, Jim,
    What is Economics? / James Eggert. -- 3rd ed.
       p.   cm.
    Rev. ed. of: Invitation to economics. 2nd ed. c1991.
    "Bristlecone books."
    Includes bibliographical references (p.   ) and index.
    ISBN 1-55934-212-9
    1. Economics.   I. Eggert, Jim, 1943– Invitation to economics.
II. Title.
HB171.E347 1992
330--dc20   92-16627
                                                  CIP

Manufactured in the United States of America
10 9 8 7 6 5 4 3 2

Bristlecone Books
Mayfield Publishing Company
1240 Villa Street
Mountain View, California 94041

Production editor, Lynn Rabin Bauer; manuscript editor, Colleen O'Brien;
text designer, Jeanne M. Schreiber; cover designer, Terri Wright; production
artist, Robin Mouat; manufacturing manager, Martha Branch; illustrator,
Willa Bower; photographs by Jim Eggert; cartoons by Robert Cavey. The
text was set in 10 1/2/13 New Century Schoolbook and printed on 50# White
Opaque by Malloy Lithography, Inc.

Preface

How interesting, indeed, how representative of our times, is the following corporate announcement from the *Wall Street Journal:*

LIBERATION CLEARS THE WAY
FOR KELLOGG PLANT IN LATVIA

Kellogg Co. says it will build a cereal plant in Riga, the capital of Latvia, to supply Russia . . . as well as the newly independent Baltic states. The plant initially will make two of Kellogg's best sellings, Corn Flakes and Frosted Flakes, probably using grains grown in the Ukraine.*

Such wide-ranging changes—political, economic, and environmental too—grab our attention almost daily; events from the large and significant to the small and intimate; from a newspaper's opening headline to concluding thoughts of a TV correspondent, or perhaps an "IMPORTANT NOTICE" enclosed in a paycheck envelope. From the international economic front to our own private economics, many of these changes will have direct or indirect implications for all of us. Fortunately, the study of economics has always provided, for students and laypeople alike, a set of reliable tools which, despite the variety of events, help us take apart, examine, and better understand the developments and issues of our times.

In addition, the economist's approach includes an analysis of resource use and resource scarcity and a way of pointing out trade-offs, choices, and costs. For example, in this third edition of *What Is Economics?,* environmental costs receive a more detailed and integrated treatment than in previous editions. Also, the end of each chapter has questions for thought and discussion and an essay box entitled "New Perspectives" that relates the chapter's material to a different point of view or expands upon some interesting aspect of an issue or subject.

One of our most important tools—supply and demand—and its real world counterpart, the *market economy,* is perhaps even more important today as Eastern Europe, Russia, and others jettison their command economies and move into a new world of markets and political democracy. Although the U.S. economy continues to be the focal point of the book, the reader will find more international connections than before.

As you read through this new edition, please keep in mind that this book is not designed to be encyclopedic in scope but is more an introduction, I hope pleasing in content and detail, with the intent of fostering, in friendly fashion, basic economic literacy. The goal is to energize students' intellects so they will want to dig deeper into this or related subjects, to pursue good books and happily discover that there's so much out there to read, enjoy, discuss, and ponder! Eventually students may gain sufficient confidence to actively participate in and creatively contribute to the major economic and political debates of the day.

As in earlier versions, a warm thanks goes to Bob Eggert—father, friend, and fellow economist. Additional thanks go to Paul Barkley, Emil Haney, Lou Tokle, Dave Liu, Richard Tyson, Bruce Pamperin, and Marty Ondrus, all of whom read parts of the manuscript and offered helpful suggestions. A special thanks goes to Professor James Pinto, colleague and author of *Study Guide to Accompany What Is Economics?* Third Edition, and to Professor Norris C. Clement of San Diego State University who made numerous suggestions on broadening the text's global perspectives. Also, I appreciate the helpful ideas from Bristlecone publisher Gary Burke and thank him for this opportunity to revise and improve the text. Pat Eggert, my wife, also supplied many new ideas and helpful suggestions throughout the process.

And finally, I can't forget all my "Intro Econ" students over the past two decades, whose individual and collective contributions have helped make this a better book in ways that would be difficult to measure.

Contents

To my father,
Robert J. Eggert

1

What Is Economics?

What Is Economics?

Unfortunately, there is no single or simple answer to this question. In the most basic sense, economics is the study of how individuals or communities survive and reproduce using scarce resources. Indeed, this definition could apply to all life forms as they pursue successful evolution over time. Using this approach, we might, for example, examine "bumblebee economics," "bluebird economics," or the complex interrelationships of a biological community, such as a prairie or rain forest.[1*]

Of course, most of our emphasis in this book will be on human societies, where economics originally meant *household management*. Still, the **economic problem** is the same: how best to use scarce resources. Household resources may include a family's money, time, communication abilities and cooperative skills, mental and physical energy, working and living space, and so on. Of course, our human objectives are much more complicated than simple survival. People have a wide variety of economic wants, including (among other things) general comfort,

---

*Notes appear on pages 215–219 in the back of the book.

financial security, interesting diversions, health, and recreational pursuits. In fact, the economic wants of most households or individuals appear for all practical purposes to be unlimited.

We are also different from other animals in that we are able to make deliberate choices as to how our limited resources will be used. Thus, a **basic definition** of economics might go something like this: *Economics is the study of how an individual or a household chooses to use limited resources to best meet its unlimited wants.*

Now let's extend our view from the household economy to the national economy. The basic economic problem is still the same: The nation's resources are limited. Our material demands, however, tend to be unlimited, and thus the nation must also, on a broad scale, try to organize its resources to best satisfy its citizens' material wants. Unwise use of resources—whether by consumers, businesses, or governments—can bring about such unfortunate results as unemployment, inflation, poverty, and (in extreme cases) hunger or starvation. The study of economics can help us understand how we can avoid the mismanagement of national resources.

National Resources

So what are our national economic resources? The first and primary resource is **labor:** the millions of men and women in the U.S. labor force (the doctor, the farmer, the computer programmer, the assembly-line worker, and so on). Labor is the *human* element in the production process.

The next national economic resource is **land.** Our land resources include every natural resource above, on, and below the soil. Air is a land resource, as is farmland and the mineral ores and petroleum in the crust of the earth. Land resources are distinguished by the fact that we cannot make more of them. The earth for example has only so much topsoil and so much oil. Once topsoil erodes away or the world's oil resources are used up, these critical land resources will be gone forever.[2]

The third national resource is **capital.** Many people think that capital means money. You often hear people say, "I need to raise (so much) capital for my new project," but what they are actually referring to is financial capital. To the economist, however, capital means the physical tools that help workers produce goods and services. In other words, **capital goods** are human made, can be reproduced or replaced, and also tend to increase the productivity of the worker.

What are some examples of capital goods? For a writer, a pencil, a typewriter, or a word processer are all capital goods. They are all tools that increase the writer's output; they are human made (unlike land resources); and, once they wear out, they can be replaced. Your pocket calculator is a capital good, and so is the car that gets you to work or school. In fact, all machinery, tools, buildings, plants, and equipment are capital resources. Now you can see that there is much more to the meaning of capital than just plain money. Obviously, capital goods are very important in determining the nation's level of wealth and overall standard of living.

Finally, we come to that elusive resource called **management.** The manager is quite special in our economy; managers coordinate and organize the other resources in order to produce and market the products and services. The reward for their coordinating abilities, their creativity and risk taking is usually in the form of economic **profit**. Failure, of course, translates into financial loss. Sometimes the manager is called an **entrepreneur;** we think, as examples, of Henry Ford and Andrew Carnegie as large-scale managers personifying this scarce resource. Perhaps the days of the great manufacturing entrepreneurs are over, but whether you are talking about the bakery down the street, Apple Computer, Sony, or General Motors, some individual or group of people must still coordinate and manage labor and capital to produce marketable products and services.

Asking Questions, Making Choices

Thus, labor, land, capital, and management are the four major resources available to produce the goods and services that people need or want in our economy. To define a working economic system, however, we must ask further questions; for example, How does an economic system determine *what* is to be produced? What will our economic output consist of and who will determine its composition? Will our economy produce bombs and tanks or hospitals and homes? Small cars, large cars, or bikes and trains? Gas, oil, or solar heat? Who or what will decide for us? Of course, different economic systems will provide different answers to these questions. Leaders in Cuba or China determine what is to be produced in a somewhat different manner than they do in the United States or Brazil.

In addition, there are other important questions to ask, such as, "How does the economic system decide *who* gets the output?" Why are incomes, goods, and services distributed in the ways they are? Throughout world history, dividing up the economic pie has often been a very controversial question. Will our economic system give a majority of the output to a few super rich families, will it try to divide the pie up more equally, or will the economic distribution fall somewhere in between? The uneven distribution of incomes and wealth often results from differences in education, intelligence, skills, work habits, monopoly power, geography, family background, luck, and political or social savvy. More equal incomes, on the other hand, are usually regulated by government policies, such as minimum-wage laws, progressive taxation, subsidized education, and welfare assistance.

And finally, there is the question *"How* will these goods be produced?" At first glance, the answer might seem to be a purely technical one. Building an automobile, for example, is a problem for the engineer. And yet we know there are really many ways to produce a finished automobile. Ideally, we want to build efficiently, using abundant, low-cost resources in place of scarce, high-cost resources. Assembling that car one way in preference to another returns us to the question of allocating resources. Choosing the correct production techniques (conserving the scarce resources and using the abundant ones) is as much an economic problem as it is a technical or engineering problem. Economics is therefore the science (or art) of making choices—of choosing the best way to organize our limited resources to meet our material needs.

Finding Answers

The method by which an economic system answers these questions varies from time to time and from country to country. In fact, there are three basic systems for organizing economic resources.

The first is called *tradition.* The decision makers in a **traditional economic system** answer these questions by saying, "We will organize our economy in the way we have always organized it," by following age-old patterns determined by a complex culture that has evolved over thousands of years. Tools and houses are constructed as they were always constructed. Junior goes into the same trade as dad, while the daughter's life will be very much like her mother's. Output is allocated by custom, with few changes over the years and generally small trial-and-error improvements over longer periods of time; tradition tends to be predictable, predetermined, and relatively static.

Economics by tradition certainly has some advantages: There may be less conflict, and there are often few expectations that cannot be met. But as an economic system, it is likely to offer a relatively low standard of living, at least as we in the industrialized world would define it. If you feel that having more economic choices moves you closer to the good life, then the traditional economic system is probably not for you.

Yet we certainly have elements of tradition in our so-called modern economy. For example, my own father is an economist, and he was once a teacher, as I am now. Many instructors still use a lecture method that dates back to Plato in ancient Greece, even though some critics think that the lecture technique should have been discarded with the invention of the computer. Whether the critics are correct or not, contemporary education certainly adheres to very traditional methods of conduct and even ritual. Women, too, have become aware of the extent to which their lives are determined by social and economic traditions. Discrimination on the basis of sex has unfortunately eliminated a large proportion of our population from competition for highly productive and professional jobs. To the extent this is true, our economy is misallocating potentially productive resources. You can probably think of many more examples of how tradition weaves in and out of our supposedly modern economy.

The second method of organizing economic resources is the **command system,** characterized by the allocation of resources, incomes, prices, and so on, by a centralized authority (in other words, a dictatorship). The command system invites no questions: Either you follow orders, or you take the consequences! This system is often the offspring of a monopoly political system; they frequently go hand in hand. The economies of Cuba and communist China are good examples, as was the economic system of ancient Egypt under the Pharaohs.

European democratic socialists believe, however, that we can have a planned, state-directed economy without dictatorship.

The combination appears to be difficult, yet some democratic state planning has been approximated in Scandinavia and Japan. The U.S. economy, too, has some elements of economic command. Our military services, for example, work on this principle, as does the government allocation of goods during wartime. When price-wage controls are in effect, we have a perfect example of government command. Furthermore, almost all government laws and regulations of economic affairs (including our tax system) constitute direction from above. By and large, however, our private enterprise system cannot really be called either a command or a traditional system.

What we have in the United States is the third mode of economic organization: a **market economy.** A relatively recent phenomenon, the **market system** motivates people by offering economic incentives and rewards within a process of exchange. Instead of government direction, decisions on resource use are made by millions of independent individuals and institutions striving to do what is best for themselves or their businesses. Here, the economic mule moves by carrot instead of stick. A market economy is indeed a system of carrots.

If the command system is centralized, the market system is decentralized. A market economy churns out prices in countless markets of supply and demand; these prices, in turn, act as guidelines in a new round of economic decisions. It is a competitive, interdependent, self-regulating system.

From a recent historical perspective, the market system appears to be the economy of choice in terms of its capacity to bring about modernization, to broaden economic opportunity, and to improve a nation's standard of living. Former communist countries, for example, such as Russia, Ukraine, Poland, Czechoslovakia, Hungary, and East Germany, have rejected political dictatorship and command economics and are moving toward democracy and a production/distribution system more in tune with a decentralized market economy. Thus, many of the large-scale, twentieth-century experiments with command economics are being phased out or abandoned outright.

Economic Sacrifices

Another way of looking at economics is to examine sacrifices— what economists call **opportunity costs.** What does this mean?

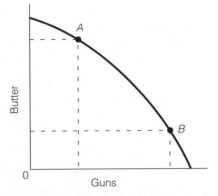

FIGURE 1-1 A society must make choices! This *production-possibilities curve* represents the various choices that society can make about military versus consumer spending. Possible combinations along the curve include a lot of butter (consumer goods) and few guns (military goods) at point *A* or a small amount of butter and a large amount of guns at point *B*.

Let's say that you have spent half an hour reading this chapter. By spending this time reading, you have given up doing a number of activities you could have enjoyed. When you use up one of your resources (an hour of time, a dollar, etc.), the cost to you is really the opportunities that you have forfeited. For example, that half hour is gone forever, and so are the alternative activities you might have enjoyed. Sometimes we hear the question, "If you had your life to live over, would you do it any differently?" If you answer yes, then you are referring indirectly to your opportunity cost.

Although this explanation of opportunity cost is somewhat philosophical, the economic concept is often more concrete. Economists look at the sacrifices that must be made when the economic resources of land, labor, capital, and management are used. If, for example, we commit our resources to producing 10 million automobiles, then these particular resources cannot be used for such alternative goods and services as housing or mass transit. Thus, the economist (unlike the businessperson) is interested not only in monetary costs but also in what is going to be sacrificed when resources are put to use.

The idea of looking at economic costs as sacrifices can be seen quite dramatically if we look at Figure 1-1. We can assume that point *A* represents an economy much like our own; it has directed most of its total resources toward the production of butter (private consumer goods) and fewer resources toward

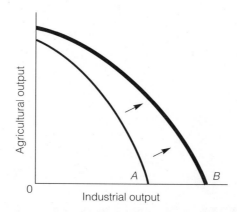

FIGURE 1-2 *Economic growth* in China is reflected by an expanding production-possibilities curve (from an early developmental stage, represented by curve *A*, to a stage of increased production, represented by curve *B*). Here, China's economic growth favors industrial output over agricultural output.

guns (military expenditures). As we move away from zero on either the guns or butter axis of this graph, we are producing more and more of that good. Thus, point *B* represents a country that has chosen to produce more military goods than consumer goods (as the United States did during World War II). Given the fact that a country has only so many total resources, it is forced to choose some mix on the line (or curve) between guns and butter. This line or curve is called the **production-possibilities curve.**

Our production-possibilities curve therefore represents all the various choices open to society regarding consumer goods production versus military production. With our limited resources, we may opt to produce more butter (*A*) or guns (*B*), but note that we cannot have large amounts of both goods—there are simply not enough total resources. In fact, to move from point *A* to point *B* means that the production of butter must be sacrificed to get more guns. Stating this opportunity cost a little differently, economists sometimes say, "There is no such thing as a free lunch."

The *true cost* (opportunity cost) is the measure of what is sacrificed. Thus, we might view the true economic cost of a large defense buildup as all the desirable things that might have been produced or accomplished if the resources had been applied to the production of peacetime goods and services. Or, the true economic cost of having so many automobiles is that the resources

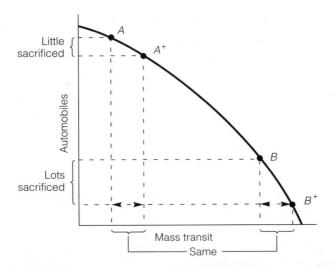

FIGURE 1-3 *Law of increasing costs:* note the *small* sacrifice (*opportunity cost*) of automobiles when mass transit increases from A to A⁺, compared to the *large* sacrifice of automobiles that results when mass transit increases from B to B⁺. The amount of increase in mass transit is the same in both cases.

used to manufacture them are not available to produce mass-transit systems (see Figure 1-3).

Now let's take a look at another production-possibilities curve. The one in Figure 1-2 represents a less-developed country like China.

Curve *A* represents the country at an early stage of development, when it has more agricultural potential than industrial potential. The expanding production curve *B* represents this country after some economic growth has occurred. The country in this example has chosen the kind of economic growth that tends to favor industrial output over agricultural output. This is a typical pattern for economic development throughout the world.

The Law of Increasing Costs

Finally, there is an additional piece of information we can gather by examining a production-possibilities curve. Take a look at Figure 1-3.

Assume for a moment that the United States is producing a lot of automobiles and few mass-transit systems; the country is therefore operating at point *A*. Now suppose that the United

States decides to put more of its resources into mass transit, so that production moves down the curve a little way from A to A^+. Note how much additional mass transit there is in relation to the relatively small amount of sacrificed automobiles. If, however, the United States is producing a lot of mass-transit systems (operating at point B) and wants even more mass transit, the country gains the same amount as before (A to A^+) when it moves from B to B^+. Note the difference in the real cost (that is, opportunity cost) of obtaining that extra mass transit: the number of sacrificed automobiles is much larger. We might say, then, that as the United States moves to higher levels of mass transit, the opportunity costs of squeezing out yet more mass transit becomes greater and greater as more and more automobiles have to be sacrificed. Obviously, when a country is producing almost all mass transit, it has few easily interchangeable resources left to switch from producing automobiles to producing even more mass transit. Thus, the sacrifice (or cost) must be very high to gain these additional trains, buses, etc. Economists call this phenomenon **the law of increasing costs.**

The Economist's Concerns

Let's return to our original question: What is economics? We might answer this question by simply saying that economics is what economists study. Most economists, in fact, are not too concerned with such broad generalizations as studying how to best allocate resources to meet our unlimited wants. They are more interested in the specific economic problems, such as unemployment, inflation, balance of payments, economic stagnation, and pollution. So we might say that economics is the study of *how society solves its economic problems.*

Alternatively, we could view economics as the study of goals—how a society moves closer to specific economic objectives. These economic goals are more or less universal; i.e., most countries of the world are striving to achieve them.

The primary economic goal, or what we might call a **successful economy,** that seems to be universally desired, is a decent material standard of living for all citizens, and much economic activity is directed toward this goal. But exactly what steps or intermediate goals might lead a country toward this end?

The first objective is *full employment*. Nations would like to see all, or nearly all, of their available resources being used. Men and women out of work, or idle machines and factories, can bring economic suffering and even social instability. It is foolish for resources to go unused when the means to correct the situation are available. How we move an economy toward full employment will be explored later in the text.

The second goal is *price stability*. Rapid price increases—what is commonly called **inflation**—have the undesirable effect of grossly distorting income distribution. The victims include savers, lenders, and people on fixed incomes; while these groups lose, others (including borrowers and speculators) win. At best, mild inflation is not terribly serious if it is accompanied by full employment. At worst, however, rapid price increases invite panic buying and may lead to the eventual collapse of a monetary system.

Conflicts arise in pursuing various economic goals, as they do in pursuing price stability and full employment. For example, when there is high unemployment, there is frequently lower inflation; however, if there is high inflation, more jobs may be available. In other words, as a society struggles to achieve one economic objective, it sometimes loses its grip on another.

The third goal is *economic growth*. Some, of course, might argue that the United States is presently overdeveloped and believe that we would benefit by not adding any more to our economic affluence.* And yet most Americans, and most other people in the world, seem to desire higher and higher levels of output and consumption. They feel concerned when the total economic output fails to rise; if output drops, alarms are sounded throughout the government and business sectors of the economy. Furthermore, in the poorest countries of the world, economic stagnation may mean hunger and possible starvation.

A fourth goal of most nations is the desire for a *quality environment*. Mounting evidence of the massive pollution problems that face our small planet compels economists to regard the environment as a major economic issue. But, again, potential conflicts can arise in pursuing these economic goals concurrently. For example, strong enforcement of antipollution laws

---

* See, for example, The pro-growth versus the anti-growth arguments on pages 104–107.

may slow down economic growth and, within some industries, increase unemployment.

A fifth goal of an economic society is to move toward a *fair distribution of income*. However, the absolutely equal distribution of income is not the objective. In a large scale market economy, perfect equality would be unrealistic and if rigidly enforced, would destroy healthy economic incentives. On the other hand, most economists would agree that a system that allows a large number of its citizens to live in debilitating poverty while others enjoy immense wealth is certainly unfair. What then can we do about a grossly unequal system?

Generally accepted methods of moving toward a more equal distribution of income include government taxation and redistribution of income (welfare, food stamps, Medicare, etc.), as well as the enforcement of equal opportunity in education and job procurement. If the government becomes, as some have suggested, the employer of last resort, then it will have an even greater impact in this area. Although some people disapprove of government intervention, the policies and programs just mentioned are at least some ways of breaking down the natural, social, and institutional inequalities that operate in all societies.

The sixth and final goal of most societies is *economic freedom*. Like the goal of fair income distribution, economic freedom is sometimes difficult to define precisely. To many people, economic freedom thrives in a decentralized, free-enterprise system in which workers choose occupations suited to their skills and experience. By this definition, twentieth-century America may be one of the most free economies in the world. Yet critics might ask what meaning economic freedom has for a consumer who has no income. Indeed, what does occupational freedom mean to an unskilled person in a high-unemployment area? How realistic would our freedom of enterprise be if you or I were to attempt to compete with Kellogg's, Shell Oil, Procter & Gamble, or the Ford Motor Company? The ideal of economic freedom is therefore often diluted by income inequalities, by barriers imposed by large, concentrated industries, and by restrictive policies and regulations of government. But compare the United States with other countries, and it's clear that the U.S. economy would score quite high in meeting many of the criteria of economic freedom.

Take a moment now to think about these six goals in relationship to yourself. How does the nation's economic performance—in terms of freedom, price stability, employment, growth, fairness, and the environment—affect you? Does the national economy help or hinder your effort to create your own personal successful economy? You can see that whether you like it or not, you are in many ways connected to the larger national and international economy.

In the next chapter, we are going to move ahead to take a more intimate look at some of the specific characteristics and inner workings of the complex system we call the U.S. economy.

Questions for Thought and Discussion

1. How are economic freedom and political freedom related?
2. Say that your grandmother gave you a 2 oz. lump of gold: What are the potential uses for the resource? Explain the opportunity cost concept using the lump of gold as an example.
3. Why would a perfectly equal distribution of income perhaps seem unfair to some individuals?
4. Why isn't money a primary economic resource?
5. How could the United States help the former communist countries evolve a genuine market economy? What are the risks and potential benefits?
6. How would you rate your state in the "quality environment" goal? Can you locate any studies or articles to document your impressions?

NEW PERSPECTIVES

A "Successful Economy" . . . What Is It?

One of the most interesting questions in economics is "What constitutes a successful economy?" Although there are conventional responses to this question (see text), there is probably no definitive answer. Indeed, you should be encouraged to think through the question yourself and perhaps come up with new and creative angles and ideas. A related question would be, "What do we mean by quality of life or a quality standard of living?" In addition, what role do our expectations and values play in a personal definition of

(continued)

a successful economy? From a materialistic point of view (both for an individual or a nation), how much is enough? And what about your success relative to others (including those in the community, the nation, and the world)?

Anthropologist Marshall Sahlins, in a somewhat unconventional view, suggests that primitive hunter/gatherer societies had a surprisingly successful economy, even a high standard of living in terms of sufficient food and a considerable amount of leisure.* At one point in his book, *Stone Age Economics,* Sahlins looks at a modern, highly consumptive economy and comments:

> Consumption is a double tragedy: what begins in adequacy will end in deprivation. Bringing together an international division of labor, the market makes available a dazzling array of products; all these Good Things within a man's reach—but never within his grasp. Worse, in this game of consumer free choice, every acquisition is simultaneously a deprivation, for every purchase of something is a foregoing of something else, in general only marginally less desirable.

Question: In regards to your own life, define a "successful economy." If you actually accomplish your goals, what will your life be like ten years from now? Fifty years? In what way will the national and international economy help or hinder your quest for your successful economy?

Question: Evaluate Marshall Sahlin's quotation above. (Before you comment, you may wish to reread the section earlier in this chapter on "opportunity cost.") In your view, is his point valid? Why or why not?

* Sahlins, Marshall. "The Original Affluent Society." *Stone Age Economics,* Chicago: Aldine-Atherton, Inc., 1972.

2

The U.S. Economy

It would not be unusual if someday someone from a foreign country asks you: "What is the U.S. economy like? What makes it tick?" How would you answer that person? In what way would you try to portray its broad outlines and significant characteristics?

Markets and Prices

We learned in Chapter 1 that the U.S. economic system is a **market economy.** Now let's amplify this important idea. A pure market economy is self-regulated, interdependent, and competitive. Self-regulation takes place when supply and demand operate for every product and service that has economic value. There is a market for welders and secretaries, for wheat and bread, for toothpicks, tractors, and teachers. Each of these interactions in turn is constantly interacting with hundreds of others. This churns out prices (or wages). These price signals modify other markets and influence economic decisions. Let's look at an illustration.

We will begin by assuming that there is a shortage of milk; and, as a consequence, the price of milk goes up. In a market economy, buyers and sellers note this signal (high milk prices) and then respond in various ways. First, the existing dairy farmers demand more cows and farmland so they can expand their operations and increase their profits. Soon, higher profits in milk production begin to attract more farmers into the dairy industry.

This growing number of farmers begins to demand more milking machines and silos. Stainless steel for milking machines and cement for silos are diverted into farming and away from other industries. Milking-machine manufacturers try to outbid steel-pipe manufacturers for the available steel. Plumbers now find that steel pipes are simply priced too high; they soon discover that low-cost plastic pipes can do the job almost as well. Suddenly the plastic industry has a need for new people and raw materials: chemists and petroleum. The many readjustments—both large and small—that could take place because of a milk-price increase are almost endless. Note that in this example no economic dictatorship tells people what to do in a pure market; things take place automatically in response to price signals in a dynamic, free economy.

In reality, our neat system of supply and demand is often not allowed to regulate itself. The government, reacting to economic special-interest groups, is often responsible for regulating the market. For example, when the federal government imposes price-wage controls, we find that prices are no longer flexible. If prices are not allowed to move upward or downward, economic signals are thwarted. Shortages and black markets develop where the demand for certain products is great. We can see something similar happening when city governments impose rent controls. When rents are artificially low, a greater quantity of rental property is demanded than is supplied, leaving many frustrated demanders. Other examples of market regulation by government include farm subsidies, minimum-wage laws, and tariffs on imports and exports. One of history's glaring examples of interference was in the former Soviet Union's controls that stifled price and wage signals for many decades. The inevitable result was economic stagnation and continuous decay in the development of consumer products and technologies. In conclusion, whenever any government interferes with the free movement of prices, whether on a small or large scale, economic efficiency is usually reduced.

Specialization

Our U.S. economy can also be described as **specialized.** Just about every worker specializes. A worker can specialize in programming computers, making handmade furniture, fixing cars, or tightening a bolt on an automobile assembly line. If we did not have such **division of labor,** many of us would be forced to become self-sufficient—like the original settlers of the American frontier—and we would undoubtedly undergo a reduced standard of living.

Why does output increase when workers specialize? Some people, of course, simply have natural abilities in some specialties. Also, the more we work at our particular job, the faster and generally more efficient we become. We learn to use shortcuts and special tools to increase our productivity. The assembly-line operation is a good example of how specialization and division of labor can create greater output than a system of nonspecialized workers.

Specialization can be worthwhile, even when an individual has superior skills in several areas. For example, Jim is a good plumber and a good mechanic. Bob is a plumber and a mechanic as well. However, Bob is almost a genius at fixing cars, whereas Jim is just average. Their skills as plumbers are about equal, but Bob is a little better here, too. Even though Bob has an **absolute advantage** in both skills, he has a **comparative advantage** only in mechanics; that is, Bob's advantage is much greater than Jim's in mechanics, but not in plumbing. Jim is not as good in either skill, but his disadvantage is smaller in plumbing. We therefore say that Jim has his comparative advantage in plumbing. If Jim and Bob lived in a town that had room for only one plumber and only one mechanic, the economy of the town would be more productive if Bob worked as the mechanic and Jim concentrated on plumbing. In short, specialization brings about higher output in almost all situations.

Some economists feel, however, that we, both as individuals and as a society, are overspecialized, despite the gains from comparative advantage. One drawback of specialization is that we become highly dependent on our specialists. What would happen if the truck drivers and railroad workers (only about 1 percent of the labor force) went on strike at the same time? Our economy would be paralyzed within a week. If the strike lasted a month, we might face starvation and panic. The slender threads of economic interdependence can easily be broken in a complex economy such as ours.

There is also some evidence that overspecialization on the assembly line and in menial jobs takes its psychological toll:

> The man whose whole life is spent in performing simple operations which the effects to are, perhaps, always the same, or very nearly the same, has no occasion to exert his understanding or to exercise his invention. . . . He naturally loses, therefore, the habit of such exertion and generally becomes as stupid and ignorant as it is possible for a human creature to become.

Adam Smith wrote this in his book *Inquiry into the Nature and Causes of the Wealth of Nations* in 1776. Even today, we see some people rebel against overspecialization. Sometimes we read, for example, of individuals or families moving from the cities into the country to set up homesteads where they try to be relatively self-sufficient. Some build their own homes, make their own clothes, grow some of their food, and cut wood for heat, as most of our nation's farmers did generations ago. Even though their material standard of living is usually lower than average, many take pride in their work and seem relatively happy with their newly found independence.

Finally, there is evidence that many people—even those with specialized jobs—would like to rely less on the services of others. Home gardening, for example, is fairly common; do-it-yourself remodeling has always been popular in this country. These trends seem to defy the laws of comparative advantage and specialization. Still, by and large, we remain primarily specialists, operating within an interdependent and highly specialized economy.

Self-Interest

If much of our productivity and efficiency comes from specialization and division of labor, the motivation to do all this work comes from **self-interest.** Why do some people go into dirty coal mines or get up early on a cold winter morning to work on an outdoor construction site? Why does the barber or hair stylist cheerfully work on your hair even when he or she isn't feeling so hot? Why does General Motors make Chevrolets? Why do some companies go to the trouble of creating a "better" fast-food hamburger or a "new and improved" paper diaper? There is no economic commander-in-chief telling them what to do, and they usually don't do these things because of tradition. They perform their jobs because it is in their own self-interest to do so. Economists sometimes call this self-interest **income** or **profit maximization;** others call it "just trying to make a living." Whatever it's called, it is the motor of our capitalist economic system. Things usually get done because each individual group or institution is constantly trying to enlarge its base of income, consumption, or profit.

The self-interest of businesses is to maximize profits. The self-interest of workers is to maximize income. And finally, the self-interest of consumers is to maximize their material satisfactions from limited incomes.

Surprisingly enough, out of this self-centered motivation, a situation where one might think economic chaos would prevail, the society as a whole benefits. In *The Wealth of Nations,* this is what Adam Smith meant by the **invisible hand** when he said that each individual (or business) pursuing his own interest is "led by an invisible hand to promote the end which was not part of his intention." [3]

It was not the intention of the diaper company to make it easier for parents to take care of their babies. The company's purpose was to make a profit. Therefore, the company had to make something society wanted. This is where paper diapers came in. If the company did not make a product society wanted, it would be eliminated by the laws of economics. You might recall this ad from the Sun Oil Company; it has a refreshing honesty about it:

> These days, I need all the friends I can get. This is a tough business I'm in. You really have to hustle to make a buck. And right now I need the bucks. I'm due for a new wrecker. A new car. And my wife's screaming for an avocado refrigerator. That's why, when you drive into my station, I'm going to come out smiling. I'm going to wash your front window. Your back window. Now to be honest, I'm not really crazy about having to work this hard, but I need that new wrecker, the new car, and like my wife says, what's an avocado kitchen without an avocado refrigerator? Try me; I can be very friendly.

Of course, not everyone is interested in maximizing his or her income. Henry David Thoreau once said, "None can be an impartial or wise observer of human life but from the vantage ground of what we should call voluntary poverty." [4] And in his thought-provoking article, "Four Reasons for Voluntary Poverty,"[5] James Park explains that income maximization can lead to exploitation, pollution, compromises on personal freedom, and a tacit support of militarism (through taxes). Readers will have to decide for themselves whether voluntary poverty is a desirable path to follow. It seems safe to say, however, that if a majority of workers and businesses renounced income or profit maximization, the U.S. economic system would be radically different from what it is today.

Private Ownership

Another notable characteristic of our economy is **private ownership.** If we were living under a socialist instead of a capitalist system, then the means of production—the businesses, factories, capital, and other resources—would be largely publicly owned.

The debate over **socialism** versus **capitalism** has been going on for years. Unfortunately, opinions are too often based on emotion rather than on factual information. Many people, for example, are convinced that socialism implies a political system that is totalitarian, ruthless, and nonlibertarian. The truth is that a political monopoly may thrive in a capitalist state (Iraq, South Korea) as well as in a socialist one (North Korea, Cuba). Again, the major difference between the two systems is that socialist businesses are owned and controlled publicly, whereas capitalist businesses are owned and controlled privately. To say much more is to confuse the issue.

Now let's consider the term **communism.** How does it differ from capitalism and socialism? According to Karl Marx, the production-distribution philosophy of communism is "From each according to his ability, to each according to his need." Surprisingly, our most communist institution is the family. In most conventional family living situations, members receive an approximately equal distribution of goods and services. Consumption is based on need instead of on productive effort; an infant, for example, doesn't work for its formula. Pure communism has been approximated by a few comparatively small groups (the Shakers* and some North American Indian

---

* See "New Perspectives" at the end of the chapter.

communities are examples), but on a large scale, pure communism doesn't appear to be very workable.

Competition

Another characteristic of the U.S. economy is **competition.**
According to proponents of the capitalist system, competition
allows the most intelligent and skillful to prevail in a dog-eat-
dog battle for survival. This is a virtue, they say, because in a
system where only the fittest and strongest come out on top, the
economic organization itself will remain strong and healthy.
Producers must make a cheaper, better product than their rivals, or they will find themselves out of business. A competitive
economy is like a grandscale pro-football game where, according
to the late Green Bay Packer Coach Vince Lombardi, "Winning
isn't everything; it's the only thing." It should be noted that some
people feel this kind of competition may be unhealthy. Educator
George Leonard, for example, writes

> The . . . argument for hot competition all the way down to nursery
> school is that competition makes winners. The argument is, at
> best, half true. It makes nonwinners, too—generally more
> nonwinners than winners. And a number of studies indicate that
> losing can become a lifelong habit.[6]

What is perhaps even more interesting is a businessman's
reaction to the suggestion that this kind of competition creates
more problems than it solves. Leonard continues:

> I once spoke to a group of top-ranking industrialists in a seminar
> session and argued that hot competition is far from inevitable in
> the future. As my argument developed, I noticed a look of real
> anxiety on some of the faces around me. One industrialist finally
> spoke up: "If there is to be no competition, then what will life be
> all about?" We would probably be appalled to discover how many
> people in this culture have no notion of accomplishment for its
> own sake and define their own existence solely in terms of how
> many other people they can beat out.

Thus, to beat out your opponent or offer a better product or
service than your rival are common ways of defining competition. Economists, however, define it somewhat differently. A
good illustration of a competitive industry in the United States
is farming, with its tens of thousands of producers who usually
don't care about what the other producers are doing! In this

definition of *pure competition,* there are really no differences between the sellers' products. For example, grade A milk is generally the same throughout the dairy industry. We never see advertisements claiming that Farmer Jones's milk is better than Farmer Brown's. Another characteristic of competition is that no single seller is large enough to set prices or to control the market. A competitive industry is thus the least concentrated of all industries. (In contrast, a monopoly is the most concentrated.)

Obviously, to be a producer in a truly competitive industry is to operate at a disadvantage. For example, the farmers' inability to control prices and their low rate of return on investment are problems that have plagued U.S. agriculture for decades. Even though competition may mean hard times for sellers, it usually gives consumers relatively low prices. Furthermore, the more sellers there are, the more potential choices the buyer has. Competition is therefore a kind of consumer's insurance policy.

Since real competition can be threatening to businesses, we see all kinds of efforts to do away with it. Sellers can sometimes lessen competition by eliminating other sellers, by erecting barriers to new firms attempting to enter the field, and by making products slightly different from those of other sellers in the industry. Keep in mind that even though a decentralized competitive market is a traditional American ideal, it is a rare sight on our economic landscape.

To summarize, we can say that industry is *purely competitive* if it has the following characteristics:

- a large number of sellers of the same product
- no single seller with any control over price
- easy entry into the industry
- relatively low profits in the long run
- no direct rivalry among sellers

Monopolies

Now let's look at the other extreme. If competition allows consumers the widest potential choice, a monopoly seller has total control over its economic kingdom. If you are a consumer and want the monopoly product or service, you must buy from the monopolist. A **monopoly** is, in short, a one-firm industry.

Are there any good examples of monopolies in the United States? Well, your local telephone company has an effective monopoly on local telephone service and, in all likelihood, your T.V. cable company has a monopoly, too. In addition, the federal government holds a legal monopoly on first-class mail. The companies that sell you electricity and natural gas are also monopolies. We call them **natural monopolies** because the market is too small to efficiently accommodate more than one seller. If, for example, your local utility already has electric power lines leading to your home, it would obviously be inefficient (and also very costly) for another firm to install other power lines. Consumers must tolerate natural monopolies; so what protects them from profit-maximizing utilities? The answer is government regulation. Although natural monopolies are legally protected, their prices and rates are usually subject to review by public commissions.

There are other monopolies, however, that operate without any restrictions. Imagine a small town with just one drug store or only one dentist. We call this kind of market a **regional monopoly.** We can't say these are pure monopolies, because there may be another dentist or drug store 20 miles away. Yet for the retired residents of that town or for people with no convenient transportation out of town, the one dentist or drug store becomes an effective monopoly. In such a situation, the buyer is (from an economic perspective) at the mercy of the seller. Did you ever have the nightmare that your car breaks down in the middle of nowhere and you discover there is just one garage within 50 miles? Perhaps you can imagine the owner of the garage rubbing his hands together as his tow truck brings your car in. Unregulated monopolies can be bad news!

We can also see monopolistic behavior among the big industrialists. American Tobacco, Standard Oil, and Alcoa Aluminum were considered monopolies at one time. Others, such as General Electric and Westinghouse during the late 1950s, simply agreed among themselves to set prices on certain products and then behaved as if they were a single monopoly. This arrangement is called a **cartel.**

However it occurs, such monopolistic behavior is illegal under the Sherman Antitrust Act of 1890, Section 2 of which reads:

> Every person who shall monopolize, or attempt to monopolize, or combine or conspire with any person or persons . . . shall be deemed guilty of a misdemeanor.

The antitrust laws were written in an attempt to reverse the natural tendency for industries to become more concentrated. The big often get bigger. Indeed, if one firm begins to dominate a market, there is a tendency for that firm to attempt to eliminate (or merge with) rivals.

Let's review the conditions for a monopoly:

- only one seller (one choice for the consumer)
- no close substitutes for the product sold by the monopolist
- usually large barriers of entry into the industry
- often higher prices (unless regulated) than in a competitive market

The one industry that fits all these conditions but still is not ordinarily considered a monopoly is the public school system. Some economists point out that the public school monopoly contains many of the undesirable features of an industrial monopoly (a no-choice situation, high costs, lack of innovation, etc.). Not only do consumers (students) have no alternative, but they also *must* "consume" the "service" whether they want to or not. Not to do so means penalties under the compulsory-attendance laws. Would less compulsion and more choice make for a better public school system? Some educators and economists think that alternative systems are worth a try.

Economist Milton Friedman, for one, has suggested a **voucher system** in which parents would be allowed to choose the kind of schooling they would like for their children. It would be something like the GI Bill for war veterans. (No one, for example, would insist that a student on the GI Bill must go to a military academy. The student would normally be able to choose any accredited school.) Under a voucher system for school-age children, one might choose to use educational vouchers for a public school, a private school, or even an apprenticeship. "Voluntary organizations—ranging from vegetarians to Boy Scouts to the YMCA—could set up schools and try to attract customers,"[7] according to Friedman. Minnesota and Wisconsin are, in fact, currently experimenting with a modified voucher system; other states are also considering it.

Oligopolies

We have not yet mentioned the most prevalent type of industrial structure in the American economy. It's not competition, and it's not monopoly. Economists call this type of industry an **oligopoly,** an industry dominated by a few firms. Think of almost everything we buy—automobiles, steel, aluminum, processed food, appliances, gasoline, etc. The companies that dominate each of these industries can often be counted on one hand.

Other major characteristics of an oligopolistic industry include:

- emphasis on *nonprice competition* (advertising, product differentiation, styling, service, etc.)
- *price leadership* (usually by the largest firm)
- great difficulty (because of barriers to entry) for outsiders to compete with established firms
- *limited choice* for buyers between a few suppliers

Look carefully at the pyramid (Figure 2-1) to see how oligopoly fits between competition and monopoly in respect to market concentration. The oligopolistic industries are quite concentrated. Indeed, they are closer to a monopoly than they are to pure competition.

One of the major features of the oligopoly is *entry barriers.* What if you decided to start a rival company in the automobile industry? What difficulties would you encounter? For one thing, you would need millions and millions of dollars just to build one assembly plant, and even if you built it, you would still be left

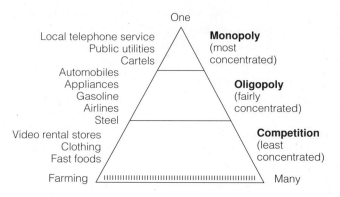

FIGURE 2-1   *Market-structure pyramid:* the upper-most point is *monopoly*—the most concentrated type of market; the base represents the thousands of suppliers that make up a *competitive market structure. Oligopoly* lies in between these two extreme market structures.

with a massive marketing problem. You would have to convince a large number of dealerships to handle your product. Even if you did that, why would people go out of the way to buy *your* car? They probably wouldn't, at least until you had established a name for yourself. This might take years and additional millions for advertising—and still would not include the high cost of financing annual model changeovers. Indeed, potential investors would probably consider your undertaking doomed to fail. Even large corporations that manufacture similar products (such as farm machinery or air frames) would hesitate to plunge into such a hazardous venture. The economic barriers are simply too great.

Well, what has happened to our model of the American economy? We began by saying that it was a competitive market economy, regulated by supply and demand. Although these concepts are still operational within our economy, we are nevertheless forced to modify some of our traditional viewpoints:

> "But aren't we now saying that much of the production in the U.S. economy is dominated by oligopolists?"
> "Yes."
> "And didn't you say that it's very difficult for a newcomer to invade oligopolistic markets because there are so many barriers?"
> "Yes."
> "Then, whatever happened to the so-called 'free-enterprise ideal'?"

"To be truthful, it's not easy to find. We do see it in local service and retail, in some innovative small-scale manufacturing (such as computer software), and above all, in the supply-demand determined industries, such as raw food and fiber and other commodities, plus the buying and selling of financial securities (stocks, bonds, etc.)."

"Supply and demand. I've heard that before. Can you go into more detail?"

"Sure. Please read on."

Questions for Thought and Discussion

1 In 1990, Iraq invaded Kuwait. Within a matter of days, the price of a barrel of oil increased by roughly 50 percent. Assuming that this magnitude of price increase had remained high permanently, list as many repercussions in the U.S. economy as you can. Include major impacts and subtle ones as well.

2. Why do economists use a "pure market economy" model if such a market does not really exist?

3 What is so natural about a natural monopoly?

4. Why is the pyramid that economists use to explain the levels of market concentration shaped the way it is?

5. List the barriers of entry that a new competitor would face in an attempt to break into the cold breakfast cereal industry. Be specific.

NEW PERSPECTIVES

"Tis the Gift to be Simple" . . . Communism in America?

Although most large-scale experiments in state socialism, or communism, have been abandoned, the idea of a small-scale communal system based on equality and sharing still intrigues some as an alternative to capitalism. For example, a physician, who specializes in the problem of aging, once wrote:

> . . . I do not want you in a nursing home . . . and I do not want you to live alone either. Women will probably continue to outlive men by more than seven years, which means that most couples

(continued)

will not survive together. There is only one solution. You have to plan for a collective lifestyle. Communes and collective houses. Now there's a pleasant thought for a grim Marxist: that the truest and best expression of communism will be forged by wrinkled hands.[8]

Actually, small-scale communistic societies were once relatively common across the American landscape. These were, of course, the religious communal experiments such as the Harmonists of Indiana, the Oneida of New York, and perhaps the best known, the Shakers, who had communities in eight states.

Nineteenth-century writer Charles Nordhoff visited a number of these communities and later summarized his views in his book *The Communist Societies of the United States 1794–1875.* In Nordhoff's opinion, those living in these societies generally enjoyed a high standard of living for their time. "I am satisfied," he wrote,

> that during its accumulation the communists enjoyed a greater amount of comfort, and vastly greater security against want and demoralization, than were attained by their neighbors or the surrounding population.*

The Shakers, in particular, seemed to enjoy a successful economy based on hard work, good management, and even technological creativity. Among Shaker inventions were the flat broom, the common clothespin, the circular saw, the air-tight stove, and the water-powered washing machine. Shakers freely shared skills and (like some Japanese workers today) enjoyed rotating jobs. Their furniture is still admired for its beauty, durability, craftsmanship, and simplicity of design. Also well known today are their songs, including one popular hymn, "Tis the Gift to be Simple." (Does the following tune sound familiar?**)

At the height of their success, Shakers had some 6000 members in 19 separate communities from Maine to Kentucky. You might someday wish to visit one of the recreated Shaker villages such as

*Nordhoff, Charles. *The Communist Societies of the United States 1794–1875* (p. 380). 1875. Reprint. New York: Hillary House Publishers, 1960.
**Music taken from *By Shaker Hands* (p. 27), by June Sprigg. New York: Knopf, 1975.

the one at at Harvard, Massachusetts, or Pleasant Hill, Kentucky, to see firsthand "communism in America" 100 to 150 years ago.

Question: What are some of the advantages versus the disadvantages of small-scale communist societies? Research one of the communities mentioned above and trace its evolution from success to eventual abandonment.

Question: Would you have volunteered to live there? Why or why not?

3

Supply and Demand

You can hardly open up a magazine or newspaper without hearing someone refer to *supply and demand:* "Lower (or higher) food prices are a result of the supply and demand for farm commodities.". . ."The U.S. housing market depends on the supply and demand for money." . . ."The future world-energy situation can be understood through supply and demand." Have you ever heard someone say that "economics is nothing more than understanding supply and demand"? An exaggeration? Yes, but not by much. So what does it all mean?

The Demand Curve

Let's begin with **demand.** To *demand* something means more than just to have a desire for a product; it implies that you want that product *and* have the money to buy it. As an example, your *effective demand* for a hamburger will be made evident only when you actually go out and buy one.

Economists are also interested in how many hamburgers people demand at different prices. By observing the quantity Q of goods bought at a variety of prices $P,$ they can work out what is called the **demand curve.** Let's look at an example.

Suppose that the price of sweet corn is $5 a bushel. Let's say that people buy five bushels at that price. If we lower the price to $4 a bushel, then they will buy, say, 10 bushels. As we continue to lower the price, observe how much more corn people will buy:

Price P ($)	$5	$4	$3	$2	$1
Quantity Q (bu)	5	10	20	30	40

This information, in turn, can easily be graphed (see Figure 3-1).

At lower prices, greater quantities are demanded. This makes sense, doesn't it? For example, when your local grocery store lowers the price of certain vegetables, you will usually buy more of those vegetables. Behind this simple economic law, however, is some interesting reasoning; let's look at what's involved.

One reason people buy more when the price goes down is that, in our example, regular buyers of corn now find that their *real incomes* have gone up slightly. Consider the Smiths—a family who likes to buy and eat lots of corn. Their *money income* has remained unchanged (the Smith's take-home pay of $500 per week is still the same), but the lower price of corn has increased their **purchasing power** (their real income). Lower corn prices mean that the Smith family can buy more of all goods, including corn, with their $500 weekly income. It's as if the Smiths were given a small income raise when they walked into the grocery store and saw that corn was marked down from, say, $0.50 to $0.12 an ear. Their greater real income probably means that they will purchase a little more of the other items they like too, such as canned tuna or flavored yogurt; but for now we are just interested in the fact that they can buy more corn. This is called the **income effect.**

The second reason people buy more when the price goes down is that they gain more total satisfaction if they buy a larger quantity of a low-priced product instead of a relatively high-priced substitute. For example, tuna and hamburger are substitute

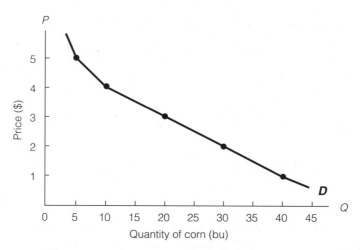

FIGURE 3-1 The *demand curve* shows that if the price of corn decreases, consumers tend to demand greater quantities of corn. This negative, or inverse, relationship between price and quantity gives the demand curve its downward-sloping appearance.

goods: they both provide protein for family meals. If they were the same price last week but tuna is much cheaper this week, consumers gain in total satisfaction by substituting the lower-priced tuna for the higher-priced hamburger. This is called the **substitution effect.**

Both the income effect and the substitution effect contribute to the economic law illustrated in our example: As the price decreases, the quantity demanded increases. Sometimes economists refer to this as the **law of downward-sloping demand,** because the demand curve does slope downward (as you can see in Figure 3-1). A downward-sloping demand curve demonstrates the inverse relationship between price P and quantity Q.

Shifting Demand

Now let's look at the demand curve from the eyes of a businessperson. As we have seen, the demand curve itself is a useful tool that shows at a glance what quantities of a product will be sold at different prices. But businesses would like to take this one step further. A business wants to see the demand curve

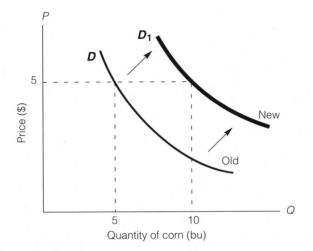

FIGURE 3-2   *Shifting demand:* at $5 a bushel, a greater quantity of corn (10 units) is demanded on the new demand curve D_2, compared to a lesser quantity of corn (5 units) demanded on the old demand curve D_1. If such increases take place at other prices, then the new demand curve appears to shift to the right, as indicated here.

for its product shift to the right, which means that even more of a product can be sold at the same price. Look, for example, at Figure 3-2; note that the new expanded demand curve D_1 shows greater quantities demanded at any given price than the old demand curve D shows.

Surely this is good for businesses—to sell more goods at a given price. But what causes the demand curve to shift? It is not a change in price, because when the price of a good changes, we simply move along a stationary demand curve D (see Figure 3-1).

What about advertising? Yes, it is commonly acknowledged that the purpose of advertising is to shift the demand curve for a product to the right and to expand its market by increasing the number of customers who buy the advertised product. Indeed, anything that brings about a broader base of potential customers will shift the demand curve to the right. For example, when the United States recognized the People's Republic of China and trade between the two countries was legalized, a new market for U.S. products, ranging from aspirin to computers, suddenly opened up.

What else might shift the demand curve? Suppose that canned peas are considered a **substitute product** for canned corn. What would happen if the price of peas suddenly went up from $0.50 to $2 per can but the price of corn remained at $0.50 per can? Corn's demand curve would increase; that is, shift to the right. The businessperson watches very carefully to see what happens to the price of substitute goods, because their price alterations can greatly influence the demand for his or her product. In summary, then, the higher the price of a substitute good, the greater the shift in the demand curve for the product that remains low in price.

If, however, two products are *complementary,* it can work the other way around. Cameras and film are **complementary products.** The demand for cameras tends to go down (the demand curve shifts to the left) if the price of film goes up. Businesses, therefore, must keep a wary eye on what is happening to the prices of those goods that go with their products.

Changes in *tastes, fads,* and *fashion* also cause demand curves to shift to the right or left (forward or backward). For example, during the late 1980s, demand for oats increased because of health concerns, and cotton products also made a comeback. Thus, consumer preference changes increased the demand for both these farm-based commodities, which in turn, increased cotton and oat prices. Also a new use for an old product shifts the demand curve to the right. A backward shift usually occurs when incomes decrease; when incomes increase, demand shifts forward. There can be exceptions, however. People in a poor family who consume lots of macaroni, for example, may experience an increase in income and reduce their demand for macaroni. Under these conditions, macaroni is considered an **inferior good.** Most goods, however, are what we call **normal goods;** an increase in income brings about an increase in the demand for normal goods.

In a free and decentralized market, a demand curve is never stationary for very long. It gets battered around like a ship in a stormy sea. An environment of rapidly changing incomes, tastes, and prices of substitute or related goods makes it all but impossible to accurately predict the behavior of the demand curve. In the more controlled markets of oligopolistic industries, the power of advertising can make demand curves more manageable and predictable than they would be in a pure market situation.

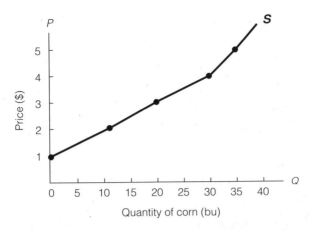

FIGURE 3-3 The *supply curve* shows that if the price of corn increases, farmers tend to supply greater quantities of corn. This positive, or direct, relationship between price and quantity gives the supply curve its upward-sloping appearance.

The Supply Curve

We now turn our attention to the **supply curve,** which shows what quantities of their products suppliers would like to provide at different prices. For example, you might ask Farmer Brown, "How much corn would you want to supply to the market if the price of corn were $5 a bushel?" Brown might reply, "At $5 a bushel, I'd supply 35 bushels." Next, you could ask what quantities he would produce at $4 a bushel, at $3, and so on. Let's say Brown gives you the following information:

PRICE P ($)	$5	$4	$3	$2	$1
QUANTITY Q (bu)	35	30	20	12	0

Based on this information, the supply curve S can be graphed as shown in Figure 3-3.

We can see that Farmer Brown's supply curve is upward-sloping: the higher the price, the more he wants to supply; the lower the price, the less he's willing to supply. In fact, at the price of $1 per bushel, Brown does not want to supply any corn at all! Other farmers will probably respond in much the same way, so we could ask all corn growers our supply question. Instead of

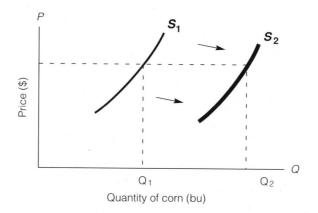

FIGURE 3-4   *Shifting supply:* when a greater quantity of a good is supplied at different prices, the supply curve shifts to the right (from S_1 to S_2).

one individual farmer producing 35 bushels at $5 each, we may find that all corn growers will supply 35 million bushels at $5 a bushel, 30 million at $4, and so on. The curve will have the same original shape, regardless of the quantities involved.

Remember how the demand curve in Figure 3-2 shifted back and forth? The supply curve can shift, too, as shown in Figure 3-4. A rightward shift in the supply curve means that a larger quantity will be supplied at a given price. This increase in supply can take place when more suppliers move into the market. If businesses move out of the industry, the supply curve often shifts to the left.

Perhaps the major reason for an increase in supply is *technological advancement.* Good examples include Henry Ford's introduction of the automobile assembly line and the development of new and improved hybrid corn seeds. Shifting the supply curve to the right (through technology) has often resulted in lower prices and the creation of mass-consumption markets. Try drawing a simple market under conditions of fixed (nonshifting) demand and supply; now shift the supply curve to the right, and see what happens to the product price.

What else can cause a shift in the supply curve? If the costs of production (for example, labor costs) go up, then the supply curve will usually shift backward (to the left). In addition, certain industries, such as farming, must always contend with supply changes caused by the weather; extreme weather conditions can

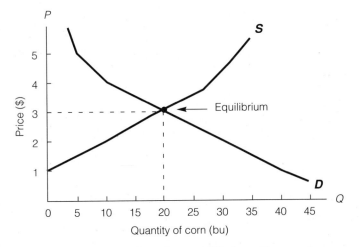

FIGURE 3-5   At the point of market equilibrium, the supply curve crosses the demand curve. The quantity demanded equals the quantity supplied only at the *market equilibrium price* ($3).

have a great impact on food commodity supply and, hence, on food prices. And so it goes. The supply curve, like the demand curve, is buffeted about by a variety of forces, some predictable, some not.

Market Equilibrium

Now we're ready to take one more important step. We have enough information to combine the supply and demand curves to form a *market*. Carefully examine Figure 3-5, a corn market created by putting our demand and supply curves in Figures 3-1 and 3-3 together on the same graph. This gives us a visual representation of what quantities of corn demanders will buy at different prices and of what quantities of corn suppliers will sell at different prices. Note that there is only one price at which the quantity supplied is equal to the quantity demanded; this is called the **equilibrium price.** According to the graph, that price will be $3 per bushel (unit) of corn. At $3 a bushel (unit), suppliers will want to offer 20 bushels of corn and demanders will want to buy the same quantity. No other price will clear the market in a similar way.

Indeed, what will happen if the price of corn is something other than the equilibrium price? To answer this question, imagine a large warehouse: on one side, we have corn suppliers; on the other, corn demanders. In the middle is the auctioneer (who is not aware of the true equilibrium price). Just to get things started, the auctioneer shouts out in a hearty voice, "Five dollars a bushel!" Can you see what will happen? At $5, the suppliers will want to sell 35 bushels, but the demanders will only want to buy five bushels (see tables on pages 31 and 35). Something is wrong! The price is too high. A surplus of corn is piling up in the suppliers' corner, while the demanders sit tight. An oversupply of corn begins to glut the warehouse. The auctioneer realizes his mistake and has no alternative but to lower the price.

Now, however, he goes to the other extreme. He yells out, "Two dollars!" Now what happens? The glut quickly disappears as the quantity of low-priced corn is eagerly bought up by demanders. After the dust settles, we find many frustrated demanders wanting large amounts (30 bushels) of $2 corn, but suppliers are unwilling to provide more than 12 bushels at that price. Again, something's wrong! The frustrated demanders start to put pressure on the auctioneer to raise the price again. After more trial and error, he arrives at the final price (the equilibrium price) of $3 per bushel.

In the *free* (unimpeded) *market* in our example, the price of a bushel of corn had complete freedom to move to equilibrium. However, in the real world, prices may not be so free. Suppose that the corn farmers (who are only a small fraction of the total voters) organize and form a political lobbying group called CORN (Corn-growers Organization to Raise Net profit). They quickly obtain hundreds of thousands of dollars, which they spend on dinners and other favors for legislators and help finance the reelection of friendly candidates. When legislation comes up regarding a **price support** for corn (sometimes called a **price floor**), the lobby works hard to get a favorable vote. After considering the bill, the legislators pass it with votes to spare. CORN reports to its members that the government will support corn prices!

So what does this mean? A price support means that the government will guarantee the corn farmers a unit price above the equilibrium price. In other words, the free-market forces will not operate while the price support is in effect. Let's look at this situation in a graph.

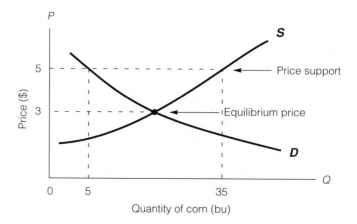

FIGURE 3-6   The *support price* (for example, $5) of a bushel of corn is a price, established by the government, that is higher than the market equilibrium price ($3) of a bushel of corn.

In Figure 3-6, we see exactly what effect this government interference will have. If the price support is $5 per unit, then 35 units will be supplied but only five units will be demanded. Clearly, the government will be compelled to buy up the surplus of corn (the difference between these two quantities) at $5 per bushel—a profitable deal for CORN! Its members can produce more corn than they would have produced at the equilibrium price and receive a higher support price for it.

But if you consider all the ramifications, there are bound to be some problems. As consumers and taxpayers, you and I will pay more for corn ($5) and get less (only five units), while we also pay more in taxes to provide these government *subsidies* to the corn growers. In addition, we will be paying even more taxes to finance the storage of the surplus. In similar examples in American industry (especially in agriculture), the taxpayers' money artificially raises prices and impedes free-market forces. This happens because when it comes to legislative support, special-interest groups usually speak with a shout, while consumers (and taxpayers) with no special lobbyists speak in a whisper.

Now let's reverse the situation. What if the government establishes a lower price for a bushel of corn than the equilibrium price? The government would in effect be telling the corn growers, "You cannot legally charge more than $2 for a bushel of corn." This \$2 price is called a **price ceiling.** What effect would this government intervention have on the corn market? Like our warehouse example earlier, the lower price will generate greater quantity demanded than supplied. The frustrated demanders want to bid up the price, but the government won't allow these prices to rise. A permanent corn shortage is therefore created. What, then, is the rationale for a price ceiling?

Sometimes the government will impose price ceilings on certain key items in an attempt to slow down inflation. But just as our example predicts, sooner or later, consumers will begin to experience shortages. In time of war, however, shortages already exist; then the purpose of a ceiling is to prevent prices from going through the roof. In the cases of necessary items (food, gasoline, fuel oil, etc.), a price ceiling may not be enough. Often, so-called **black markets** are created in which the price of a product is bid up illegally. (Never underestimate the power of the market!) When black markets develop, one potential solution is to allocate scarce commodities, using ration tickets or stamps. Rationing, however, needs an expensive bureaucratic support system, and black markets in ration tickets or stamps may develop. No matter how they are handled, price ceilings usually turn out to be political nightmares.

Shifting Supply and Demand

Even if we assume that government price interference has been abolished, prices still may change due to shifts in supply and demand. For example, as shown in Figure 3-7, after a period of wartime economic austerity, a rapid increase in the supply of a product can come about when new suppliers enter the market or when the industry experiences some rapid technological advancement. This increase will shift the supply curve to the right (from S_1 to S_2). The equilibrium price will eventually decrease because of competition, and emergency measures to handle the shortage will no longer be necessary.

On the other hand, if the supply curve shifts to the left, prices will rise. This is what happens when, for example, bad weather reduces the supply of a farm commodity (assuming the demand curve remains stationary).

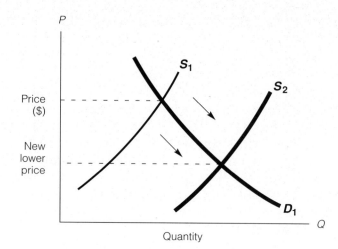

FIGURE 3-7   When the supply curve shifts to the right from S_1 to S_2 (with no change in demand), the equilibrium price is reduced.

Remember, though, that demand often is not stable for very long either. Recall that demand curves can move backward or forward for the following reasons:

- changing incomes
- a change in the price of a substitute or complementary good
- a change in taste
- advertising
- a change in the number of buyers

What will happen to the equilibrium price if there is an increase in the demand for a product? Figure 3-8 shows us. You might find it interesting to examine the commodities page in the business section of your daily newspaper. See how rapidly the prices of corn, wheat, soybeans, and other commodities can change on a daily or weekly basis because of shifts in supply and demand.

Elasticity

Another important idea associated with demand is **price elasticity.** Let's consider a practical example. A restaurant owner

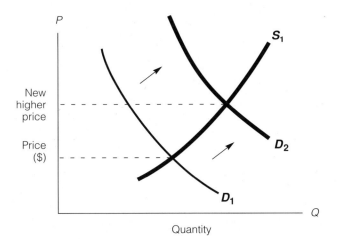

FIGURE 3-8   When the demand curve shifts to the right from D_1 to D_2 (with no change in supply), the equilibrium price is increased.

charges $5 for a top-quality small pizza. Not long ago she was asking people if the price should be raised to $6. Of course, nobody knew for sure, but some did know enough to ask her, "Approximately how many fewer pizzas would you sell if you raised the price by $1?" They felt the answer to this question would help them get an idea of the pizza's price elasticity. It would be nice, for example, if the owner could increase the price without losing any customers. On the other hand, the owner could lose a great deal of customers. Two possible demand curves for these small pizzas are shown in Figure 3-9.

Although the demand curves in (a) and (b) are downward-sloping (remember our law of downward-sloping demand?), the curve in (a) is much flatter than the curve in (b). To put it another way, the demand curve in (b) is much steeper than the curve in (a). If (a) represents the demand curve for small pizzas, would it be wise to raise the price? Probably not. Economists would say that this is an **elastic demand curve** (the quantity demanded is very responsive to a change in price). In (a), even with a small change in price, we see the quantity of pizza demanded decline rapidly to less than one half of what it was. Businesses intending to raise their prices would probably rather have a demand curve like the one in (b), because they can increase the prices of their products without losing much quantity

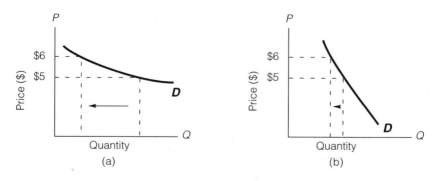

FIGURE 3-9   In graph (a), a $1 increase in price (from $5 to $6) reduces the quantity demanded by a considerable amount. This demand appears to be *elastic*. In graph (b), the same $1 price increase reduces the quantity demanded by only a small amount. This demand curve is *inelastic*.

demanded. Economists call this an **inelastic demand curve** (the quantity demanded is not very responsive to a change in price).

What kind of products have inelastic demand curves? One example of an **inelastic good** is table salt. If salt is $0.30 a box but then doubles in price, people will still demand about the same amount of salt. However, if new cars became twice as expensive, there would probably be a fairly large reduction in the number of cars demanded. New cars are therefore an example of an **elastic good.**

Let's examine a few other examples. Gasoline and toy balloons are inelastic goods. The prices on both of these items could be increased substantially, and in the short run, demand would not be greatly reduced. Can you see a pattern that might allow you to predict the degree of elasticity of a product? Why are some goods sensitive to a change in price whereas others are not? Some general principles for determining *inelastic* demand might include the following:

- It's a necessary good (gasoline, heating oil, prescription drugs, telephones).
- It's a small part of the person's budget (toy balloons, soda pop, paper clips).
- There are few substitutes (insulin, light bulbs, diamond rings).

Note that table salt meets all of these criteria. No economic good, however, is necessarily inelastic at all prices. If we walked into the grocery store and discovered that the price of salt was not $0.30 or $0.60 a box but $10 a box, the quantity demanded would be greatly affected! In this case, you would probably learn to eat your food with less salt (or use a salt substitute), and your favorite restaurant would sell you small salt packets instead of putting a salt shaker on the table.

Let's get back to the pizza restaurant. The relative **elasticity of demand** for the pizzas will depend mainly on how many substitutes (both direct and indirect) are available. A *direct substitute* would be a Pizza Hut restaurant down the street; an *indirect substitute* might be cooking a pizza at home. If the restaurant owner happens to be a monopolist and people regard eating pizzas out as a necessity, then a price increase more than likely will benefit the business.

Is there any way that the restaurant owner can affect the elasticity of demand for her pizzas? Yes, if she can convince people that she has a truly unique, superior, and necessary product. Note the words "if she can convince people"; she does not necessarily have to have a better or different product.

Advertisers for Bayer aspirin, for example, try to convince people that their product is truly different. Most druggists say that aspirin is aspirin, but by convincing aspirin users that Bayer is superior, the company has successfully made its product demand curve more inelastic than it would otherwise have been; hence, the company is often able to charge a higher price than its competitors.

Our theory still does not enable the restaurant owner to determine whether the demand for her pizzas is elastic or inelastic. The only way to know for sure is to actually raise the price and see what happens to sales (*total revenue*). We can say with some accuracy that if you increase the price and the total revenue goes up, the demand between these two prices is inelastic; if you increase the price and the total revenue is reduced, the demand is elastic. Let's call this the *businessperson's definition* of price elasticity.

Note that the demand in Figure 3-10(a) is inelastic. It should be apparent that the lower-price total revenue (price multiplied by quantity) is quite small. To tell for sure, simply

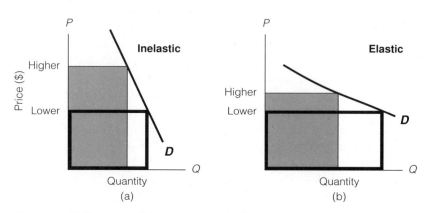

FIGURE 3-10 In graph (a), demand is *inelastic:* increasing the price tends to increase total revenue. The shaded block, which represents total revenue, is somewhat larger than the total area within the thicker, black lines. In graph (b), demand is *elastic:* increasing the price tends to decrease total revenue. The shaded block is somewhat smaller than the total area within the thicker black lines.

compare the area that represents total revenue at the lower price (the area inside the thicker black lines) with the shaded area of total revenue at the higher price. By raising the price in the inelastic example, total revenue is increased. This is, of course, what the restaurant owner wanted to happen when she raised the price of her pizza. Note what would have happened if demand had been elastic. In Figure 3-10(b), we see that the increase in price reduces the quantity demanded so much that the total revenue (shaded area) becomes smaller compared to the area inside the thicker black lines (lower-price total revenue).

A final point to remember: If you are a businessperson, it might be in your best interest to lower prices, particularly if your demand curve is elastic. A lower price on an elastic demand curve will generate so much more business that total revenue will go up. In addition, expanding the scale of business operations will often lower the *unit cost of production.* If unit costs go down as the operation gets larger, economists say that the business is taking advantage of **economies of scale.** After World War I, Henry Ford combined these two ideas (an elastic demand for cars plus mass-production efficiencies) and reaped a personal fortune of over a billion dollars. It pays to know about elasticity!

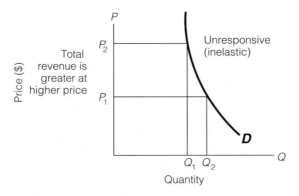

FIGURE 3-11 This exaggerated inelastic demand curve clearly shows a higher total revenue (larger rectangle) at the higher price than at the lower price.

Now let's take a moment to review what we have learned about this subject. Elasticity is basically a measure of how much the quantity demanded responds to a change in price. An elastic curve is very responsive to price variations; an inelastic curve is not very responsive.

Elasticity can also be determined by observing what happens to total revenue (or total sales) when the price changes. If total revenue goes up when we raise the price, we have *inelastic demand.* If total revenue goes down, we have *elastic demand.* If you find yourself confused about what happens to total revenue when the price is changed, simply sketch an exaggerated demand curve (either very flat or very steep) and see what happens to total revenue when the price goes up or down (for example, see Figure 3-11).

So far, so good, but we still do not know how to determine the precise degree of elasticity. For example, both salt and gasoline are inelastic goods, but which is more inelastic?

Let's suppose that the President of the United States determines that gasoline supplies may be threatened and decides that it is in the national interest to reduce the nation's consumption of gas by 15 percent. There are, of course, different ways to handle this situation. First, he might ask drivers to reduce their consumption voluntarily. If this doesn't work, he could establish a gasoline rationing system. We know, however, that this kind of rationing invites black-market counterfeiting and requires an expensive bureaucracy to make it work.

The third and probably the quickest way to reduce consumption would be to raise the price of gasoline to the consumer via a tax increase. But how much would the total price of a gallon of gas have to go up in order to reduce by 15 percent the quantity of gasoline demanded? Would a 15 percent increase in price do the trick, or a 30 percent increase, or perhaps even a 75 percent increase? This question leads us to our most exact definition, the *economist's definition of price elasticity*.

To measure the precise value of a product's elasticity, we divide the percent change in price into the percent change in quantity demanded:

$$E_p \text{ (coefficient of elasticity)} = \frac{\text{Percent change in quantity demanded}}{\text{Percent change in price}}$$

If this ratio is greater than 1, it is elastic; if this ratio is less than 1, it is inelastic. For example, if we find out that the price of a gallon of gas must increase by 30 percent to reduce gasoline consumption by 15 percent, then the exact elasticity of a gallon of gas would be:

$$E_p = \frac{15\%}{30\%} = 0.50$$

Since this ratio is less than 1, it's inelastic. If the President had known beforehand that the coefficient of elasticity for gasoline was 0.50, he would have known exactly how much gasoline prices would have to increase before consumption would decrease by the desired amount.

As another example, let's assume that the demand for pizzas is very elastic. The restaurant owner goes ahead and raises the price of a pizza by 20 percent anyway and discovers that the quantity of pizza demanded goes down by 80 percent. Under these conditions, what is the elasticity of demand? Using our formula, the answer would be:

$$E_p = \frac{80\%}{20\%} = 4.0$$

This ratio is greater than 1, so the demand is elastic.

In the real world, you may never know the exact elasticity of a product. It may change over time, or it may be one value in a lower price range and a totally different value in a higher price range. Still, the most successful businesspeople seem to have an uncanny instinct for elasticities and how they affect revenues and profits.

Now what about you? What products do you buy? How elastic or inelastic are they to you? If the price of your favorite newspaper or magazine were raised considerably, would you still buy it? Would you buy your favorite hamburger or pizza if the cost went up 20 percent or 30 percent? These are the kinds of interesting economic questions we can all ask ourselves.

In summary, we have come a long way in understanding the inner workings of an individual market. We have discovered how supply and demand operate and how the natural forces of the market drive prices toward an equilibrium price. We have also seen what happens when these natural forces are impeded by price supports and price ceilings. We now know that the supply and demand curves shift in response to a variety of economic forces and also know how such information can be of value to consumers, businesspeople, and government.

So we've learned quite a bit about single markets; but what about the vast interconnections between these single markets and the overall economy? What about the massive amounts of money, goods, and resources flowing in and out of millions of household and business markets? How does all this fit together to form an economic system? We are now ready to find out.

Questions for Thought and Discussion

1. How could the concept of elasticity be used to establish government policy?

2. Do the concepts of supply and demand apply only to conventional private production and private consumption? Or can they be applied to nontypical areas of consumption, such as prostitution, drugs, crime, etc? Explain.

3. Does the existence of an equilibrium price and an equilibrium quantity mean that all suppliers and demanders are

willing to produce and consume at that point of balance? Why or why not?

4. Why do we need the concept of elasticity when we can just look at the slope of the demand curve to determine how price affects quantity demanded?

NEW PERSPECTIVES

Russian Econ 101 . . . The Problem of Pricing

The stage is set.

Imagine for a moment that you live in Moscow and that your country, Russia, has just embarked on a bold and controversial economic experiment. Time? Early 1992. Your President (Boris Yeltsin) has signed into law a directive that would pave the way for private ownership of businesses and also abolish government pricing of goods and services.

The ultimate objective is nothing less than transforming a rigid command economy into a competitive, decentralized, free-market economy. The success of Yeltsin's new economic plan will, on the one hand, depend upon a quick relinquishment of the old, that is a weaning of producers from government dependency and centralized decision making; and on the other hand, fostering a multitude of private interactions based on market—incentives including the lure of profits, the sprouting of entrepreneurs, and a new respect for Adam Smith's "Invisible Hand."

You may ask, "What was wrong with the old system?" Among the many problems was that of pricing; i.e., how the central government could set a price consistent with demand and supply while taking into consideration the abundance (or scarcity) of resources. Columnist William Murchison succinctly stated the dilemma when he wrote:

> Without free prices, no one can gauge demand; no one knows how much of something to make, or what materials to use in it, or where to sell it, or how much to pay the work force. Shortages and misallocations are inevitable under centralized control. It's like ping-pong in a root cellar at midnight.*

For political reasons, prices in the old command economy tended to be ceilings: Legal prices set *below* what would prevail in a free market (see page 41). Price ceilings diminish the incentives to produce yet encourage greater consumption. Small wonder that consumers had to wait in long lines in response to the inevitable

* Murchison, William. "Yeltsin's Economic 'Gamble' a Sure Thing." *The Arizona Republic,* January 7, 1992.

shortages! Later when prices were allowed to seek their market equilibrium level, supply/demand theory would predict that, in the short run, the cost of goods would tend to rise.

Question: Did the theory match reality after Yeltsin abandoned price controls in early 1992? (Check your library for information.) Also, outline the long run problems of evolving a market economy. Consider, for example, the need to create credit institutions, a stock market, a legal base for private property, business schools, private research facilities, etc. Can you list anything else?

Question: Can you draw a supply/demand graph showing an eventual lowering of prices in the Russian economy? (Hint: Review Figure 3-7 and the factors that would bring the desired change.)

4

Businesses and Households

We are now ready to take a larger view of our economy. In this chapter we will enlarge our economic vision to include not only the single supply-demand markets discussed earlier but also the major economic institutions of businesses and households that give life to these individual markets. Instead of using an economic microscope to focus on a particular market, we now need a pair of wide-angle binoculars to help us see the broad outlines of our large and complex economy.

Let's begin with an analogy. The operation of our economy is something like the operation of an automobile. The performance of both depends on two vital flows. On the one hand, gasoline (the automobile's primary operating resource) flows from the gas tank through the carburetor into the cylinders where, on combustion, it produces power to run the car. On the other hand, a circulating flow of lubrication oil travels around and around to various parts of the engine, reducing friction in the bearings and pistons. Take away either of these two flows and the automobile will soon stop functioning.

Economic Flows

Our economic system also depends on two vital flows. The first is the flow of *money,* which economists consider a kind of lubricating agent because it makes economic exchange simpler and smoother. Money flows through resource markets (land, labor, capital), into the pocketbooks of householders, and then back into the markets for goods and services, bubbling up in the business sector. This continuous circulatory stream of money flows on and on, unless of course some aspect of the economic system breaks down.

The second vital flow are the *real* components of a dynamic economic system—actual goods and services, plus the physical land, labor, and capital needed to produce them. Real things also flow through the markets, pushed on by monetary impulses in response to levels of supply and demand, and eventually become used up or consumed.

It's a fascinating system. Let's look at a graphic representation of our economy. Figure 4-1 is a visual model of our economy that economists call the **circular flow diagram.** First note that the clockwise flow is money. Starting, for example, in the upper left corner, we find dollars flowing out of businesses (expenses) into the resource markets. There, these dollars are translated into the demand for land, labor, and capital.

When the resources are sold to the business sector, the so-called expense dollars are suddenly translated into *incomes* for the households. These dollars then flow out of the households into the markets for goods and services; we look at these same dollars and now call them *expenditures.* Demand then stimulates supply in the product (goods and services) markets. As payments are made for corn, car repairs, or bicycles, the dollars become *sales* for businesses, providing them with financial capital to start another round of productive flow. And the cycle begins all over again.

It sounds like a simple, foolproof system, doesn't it? The chance of a breakdown does exist however. For example, there is no guarantee that the *quantity of money* will be in balance with overall spending. If, for example, the money supply is too low, the economy may slow down because there is not enough currency to make basic transactions. On the other hand, too much money will create an inflationary situation where too many dollars are chasing after too few goods. Similar problems can arise when there is also too little or too much spending.

Whose responsibility is it to watch these flows and correct them if they are out of balance? The responsibility lies primarily

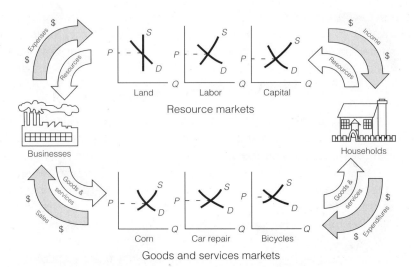

FIGURE 4-1   This circular-flow diagram is a simplified version of a market economy. Note that the two major economic sectors (businesses and households) are connected by flows and markets—the resource markets (land, labor, and capital) and the goods and services markets.

with the **government sector.** Along with the business and household sectors, government also plays an important role in the operation of our economic system. (We will have much more to say about government in Chapter 5.) For now, however, let's take a close look at the **business sector.** For example, how do we define a business? How are businesses organized? How effectively do they operate in a capitalist setting?

The Business Sector

There are approximately 20 million businesses in the United States. The majority of them are small retail or service businesses and other single-owner operations, including farming. Operating these small enterprises often means overworking "Mom and Pop" to keep the business going. To make things worse, broad statistics tell us that many small independent businesses frequently end in bankruptcy. (Three out of five new businesses fail before the third year of operation!)

Now let's play a little game. Assume that you have carefully considered the odds and have decided to plunge into a new business. You might try to write, publish, and market your own book, for example. Or perhaps you would like to manufacture computer software or run a candy store. A repair service or free-lance photography are further possibilities. For our purposes here, though, let's assume you go into manufacturing.

Of course, the first question is, "What are you going to make?" You don't want to compete with a large, oligopolistic industry because you would have to overcome large barriers to enter the market (see Chapter 2). Obviously, you want to de-velop some new or improved product. You may also wish to select something that can be manufactured by one or two people.

One day you read in *The Wall Street Journal* that the sale of cat food has quadrupled in the last decade. You begin to think

> Yes, about half my friends have cats, and you know, their cats always want to be let in or out. Why couldn't I make an entrance-exit device to let cats enter or leave the house whenever they want. It would have to be designed so that heat is not let out, and it would also have to be easy to install. . . .

You convince yourself that you can make a go of it and begin to work on a prototype. By the end of the year, you have your cat-loving friends trying out your new invention—KITTYOUT.

Now you need to think about the business end of your operation. You have several options. You may decide to set up what is called a **single proprietorship.** The proprietorship is perhaps the most simple type of business organization. It can be started up with a minimum of red tape; no charters, meetings, or extensive reports are needed. "A good deal," you say to your-self—until you find out some of the disadvantages. If you decide to expand your small operation later, you may find that no one wants to loan you any money. You try the local banks; they smile pleasantly and say, "Sorry." The Small Business Administration (an agency of the federal government) also lends a kindly ear but tells you that the enterprise is still unproved: "Come back when sales and earnings have demonstrated more promise," they say.

You can also face the disadvantage of **unlimited liability,** which means that if things go badly, your creditors can sue you not only for your business assets but also for your personal assets. For example, your child's education fund could be liqui-dated as a result of a bad business decision!

But business is going OK for now, and your major worry at present is finding the financial capital to expand. You begin thinking of alternatives, and one comes to mind: a partner. You invite a friend (or relative) to join you and form a **partnership** in order to provide additional financial capital as well as a helping hand. There is now, however, more red tape. A partnership is a legal entity, and if your partner leaves you (or dies), you usually have to start all over. Plus, you are still faced with the problem of unlimited liability.

Nevertheless, let's assume that you and your partner are not worried much about the liability problem; current sales are excellent; indeed, you both are becoming intoxicated with visions of unlimited profits. Expansion is the main concern on your minds. So you ask yourselves, "How should we expand?"

You might, for example, elect **vertical expansion.** Perhaps you have been purchasing supplies from a local sheet-metal shop, and you now decide to buy the shop out. By expanding vertically, you are *taking over another stage of production.*

Or, instead of taking over the early stages of manufacturing, you might go to the other extreme of marketing the product and set up your own shops to sell KITTYOUT. Until now, you have been selling your cat doors to a regional distributor, who, in turn, sells them to established retail shops. (In the larger economy, the oil industry is a good example of vertical expansion. It often owns or controls almost all stages of production: oil wells, pipelines, refineries, and, of course, distribution through local service stations.)

Another option is **horizontal expansion.** This means *doing more and more of the same operation.* You might buy out the competition, or you might set up a small-scale factory in another location. Either way, your expansion activities would concentrate on the assembly stage.

Another choice open to you is expansion by **diversification**—bringing out one or more additional products. They may be related to your original product, or they may be totally different products. For example, you might decide to manufacture an improved cat or dog house, or even a DOGGYOUT (based on the same design and engineering principles used in your successful KITTYOUT).

Many large American corporations diversify so widely that there is often little or no relationship between their products. A business that expands through buying or merging with unrelated businesses is called a **conglomerate.**

Why would a company diversify—especially in the direction of an unrelated conglomerate? Some say that broad diversification is more often than not a personal power trip or an exercise in financial empire building. Another answer is that large-scale, diversified companies can more efficiently disperse their overhead (the continuing costs of running the business) over all operational phases. A small company for example might not have sufficient resources to afford a business economist, a market researcher, or an advertising division, but the large parent company can afford these important marketing aids and provide such assistance when it is needed. Diversification is also a kind of insurance policy against a sudden shift in demand away from a single-product line such as vinyl recordings (replaced by tapes and compact discs) or cigarettes (consumption reduced because of health concerns). And, undoubtedly, there have been cases of diversified mergers or **leveraged buyouts** (LBOs), sometimes financed by so called "junk bonds," which have forcefully dislodged inefficient management teams and thereby improved the performance of the weaker company.[9]

There can, however, be a darker side to the trend toward mergers and leveraged buyouts. Giant companies often operate with a kind of cold, insensitive detachment. Owners of these mega-businesses may be obsessed by short-run rates of return or on selling assets for immediate profit. They can play with the fates of factories and employees with the ruthlessness of a master chess player, doing whatever is necessary to win the game. Economist Ernest Mandel captures this feeling of absentee ownership in his prophetic piece, "Where Is America Going?":

> They retain ultimate power—the power to open or to close the plant, to shut it in one town and relaunch it 2000 miles away, to suppress, by one stroke of their pens, 20,000 jobs and 50 skills acquired at the price of long human efforts.[10]

But we've gotten a little ahead of ourselves. Our KITTYOUT business is only a partnership, not a large conglomerate. The major question facing our enterprising partnership is still, "How can we best grow?"

At this stage of development, the likely answer to this question is to form a **corporation.** Among the major advantages of a corporate form of ownership are the new opportunities that are available for obtaining financial capital. A corporation, for example, can sell equity (ownership) stock as well as float corporate

bonds. In addition, obtaining a loan from established financial institutions (banks, credit unions, etc.) is often easier for corporations than for unproven single proprietorships or partnerships. **Limited liability** is another advantage of the corporate form; the debts of the corporation are limited by law to extend only to the corporate assets—not to the assets of the owners (as in a proprietorship or a partnership).

You and your partner therefore hire a lawyer to draw up a charter, and various friends and relatives buy into your little company. Thus, KITTYOUT, INC. (incorporated), joins the ranks of the approximately 3 million corporations that currently exist in the United States. However, your little company is not yet in the big time, and it probably never will be. As we discussed in Chapter 2, it is extremely difficult to create a new industrial company in an existing oligopoly industry.

To get an idea of just how big some of these giant companies can get, imagine a list of 3 million corporations, with the larger companies at the top and the smaller ones at the bottom. If we were to tally up the assets of the 200 largest corporations at the very peak of this list, we would discover that this small group of companies (less than one tenth of 1 percent) own over 50 percent of all manufacturing assets in the country! These corporations indeed dominate the mainstream of American business.

In our KITTYOUT example, we have looked at the different forms of business enterprises and noted some of their advantages and disadvantages. However, we have not yet examined the inner workings of a business. How do businesses combine their resources to produce goods and service? What rules, if any, do they follow to achieve the best results? Returning again to small-scale business, let's look at some fundamental principles.

Diminishing Returns

One well-known law of economics that businesses must be aware of when they combine resources is the **law of diminishing returns.** What exactly is this law all about? It's best to explain it with a simplified illustration.

A few years ago, I helped a neighbor, a farmer we'll call Chester Olson, bring in his hay. Chester has just one tractor, one hay baler, and one hay wagon; we call these his **fixed inputs.** His **variable input** is labor: He can choose to work by himself or with any number of hired hands. Chester told me that if he works by himself, he can bring in only two loads of hay per working day. He brings in so few loads because he has to bale the hay, pick it up off the ground, stack it on the wagon, unload it from the wagon into the barn, and then climb up into the hot, sticky hay and stack it neatly—a big job for one man.

If I help Chester, the total output per day goes from two to five loads. My additional contribution, sometimes called the **marginal physical product** (MPP), is three full loads of hay above what Chester can bring in by himself. Because a second person (myself) increased *per worker output,* we can say that Chester is in a stage of **increasing returns.** But if we add a third person (Steve), we find that total output goes up only one additional load to make six total loads. With Steve added to the production force, total output goes up, but at a *diminishing rate.*

Beginning with Steve (the third person), we have apparently reached the **point of diminishing returns.** Why did it begin with Steve? Is he lazy? Definitely not. If Chester or I had been that third person, the same thing would have happened. The reason diminishing returns begins with Steve is because Chester has a *fixed set of machinery* for us to work with. If Chester had additional equipment—perhaps just one more hay wagon—that third person might give us a lot more loads. When we speak of diminishing returns, we therefore must assume that *all inputs except one are fixed.*

How will this knowledge of diminishing returns help Chester make decisions concerning the number of people to hire? Can we automatically assume that Chester shouldn't hire that third person? If Chester is a good businessperson, he should take a

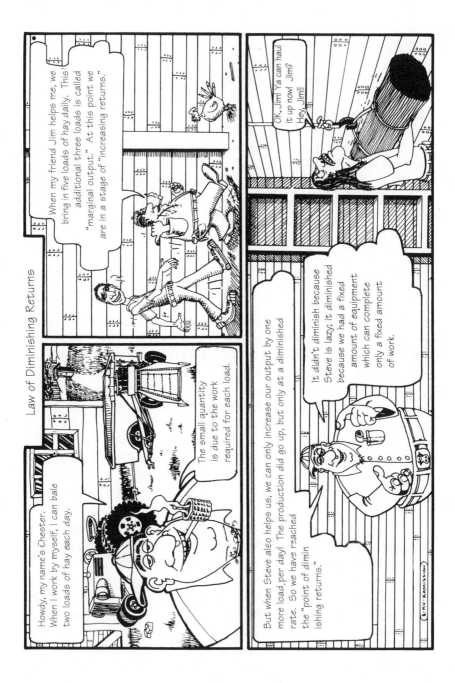

Howdy, my name's Chester. When I work by myself, I can bale two loads of hay each day.

The small quantity is due to the work required for each load.

When my friend Jim helps me, we bring in five loads of hay daily. This additional three loads is called "marginal output." At this point we are in a stage of "increasing returns."

OK, Jim! Ya can haul it up now! Jim?

Hey, Jim!!

But when Steve also helps us, we can only increase our output by one more load, per day! The production did go up, but only at a diminished rate. So we have reached the "point of diminishing returns."

It didn't diminish because Steve is lazy; it diminished because we had a fixed amount of equipment which can complete only a fixed amount of work.

careful look at how much extra money the third person's extra loads of hay will bring and compare it with the cost of hiring him. To illustrate, if the value of an additional load is $50 and Chester has to pay Steve only $20 to bring in the load, then it would be profitable to hire Steve despite the law of diminishing returns. The general rule is to *keep hiring people as long as the value of the marginal product* (the additional hay) *is greater than the cost of producing that product* (the extra wages Chester must pay to get the additional hay).

Chester has it quite easy. Besides keeping his old baler running, all he has to worry about are diminishing returns, the price of hay, and the cost of hiring an extra hand. Imagine, however, the complex decisions that must be made concerning the production of something as complicated as an automobile. How would you go about finding the ideal mix of resources to manufacture a car?

Perhaps the best way to build a car might be to simply give an engineer the following proposal: "Here is our design; tell us how to build it!" A good engineer, however, should come back with more than one solution: "Here is one way to build your car that is almost completely mechanized; here is another method that is more labor intensive (uses more human labor)." The engineer may go on to tell you many other different ways to build approximately the same car. The bumpers might be made of plastic or steel; the engine block of cast iron or aluminum. In fact, an engineer may give you an entire book describing possible techniques that meet your design specifications. How do you choose?

The answer, of course, is that for any given product, you should choose the lowest-cost technique. If you don't, your rivals may—and then you might find yourself out of business. When businesses choose the lowest-cost technique, note that the entire economy will become more efficient. Returning to the idea of supply and demand, the ideal approach is to conserve the most scarce resources and use the most abundant ones. If a resource is scarce, its supply will be low; if it is in demand, the resource will command a high price. In trying to minimize production costs, businesses will naturally avoid using that scarce resource.

Abundant resources, on the other hand, tend to cost less in the marketplace. A business will therefore choose these plentiful, low-cost resources more and more often. It's a simple idea when you think, for example, of how much more low-cost plastic is being used in the place of relatively high-priced steel or wood. Consumers, in turn, benefit from relatively low-cost products.

In summary, *low cost equals economic efficiency*. This constant drive to lower cost is indeed one of the most remarkable and beneficial characteristics of a capitalist economic system. Ironically, it is one of the most destructive aspects of our economic system as well. Why is this so?

Pollution

The drive to operate businesses at the lowest cost possible has also contributed to the pollution problem. Take, for example, Gary, Indiana. If you have ever driven past the steel and oil production complex in Gary, you probably had to close your car window. The air is often unbearably dirty. Why do these companies pollute the air? Do they want to increase the death rate and the incidence of lung disease? Obviously not. They pollute the air and water for a simple reason: it's cheaper to pollute than not to pollute.

Of course, in almost every such case, there is a technology available that will reduce pollution to reasonably low levels. However, if they can get away with it, why shouldn't producers attempt to push the clean-up costs onto society (that is, make them **social costs**) instead of paying these costs themselves? Thus, in a strange way, our economic system tends to reward polluters: the more pollution (without incurring any penalties,) the lower your costs and, hence, the greater your profits. In a few instances, when short-run profit making is pushed to an illogical extreme, the attitude and actions of a company can be difficult to believe:

> "Profit-ability" was the 1970 slogan for Union Camp, a company whose paper-bag plant helps make the Savannah River one of the foulest sewers in the nation. The executive vice-president of the company, answering Nader's Raiders' charge that his firm was dangerously depleting groundwater supplies, replied, "I had my lawyers in Virginia research that, and they told us that we could suck the state of Virginia out through a hole in the ground, and there was nothing anyone could do about it." Union Camp's director of air and water protection noted for the benefit of *The New York Times* that "it probably won't hurt mankind a whole hell of a lot in the long run if the whooping crane doesn't quite make it. . . ."[11]

Fortunately, most businesses today cannot operate with such total disregard for the environment. Nonetheless, the short-run pressures to keep costs down continue to create problems in our economy. In fact, this is what we might now call the **first tragic flaw of capitalism:** In the great drive to be efficient producers, which lowers production costs and generally benefits the consumer, we have simultaneously provided an irresistible temptation to pollute. What can be done about this problem?

In theory, the economic remedy is quite simple: Force producers to pay *all* production costs. *Neighborhood effects*—passing pollution costs on to society at large—should not be tolerated. Perhaps the easiest way to enforce this rule is to impose a pollution tax. The government would be saying, in effect,

> Until now, you have behaved as if the air and water were a free resource—a free trash can that never fills up—but from now on, you will have to pay a pollution tax for the use of that trash can. In fact, we will make the tax so high that it might be more profitable for you to buy your own garbage cans and collect your pollutants yourself.

A more direct approach to the pollution problem is to state maximum levels of pollution (as the government has done with automobile emissions). Yet there are drawbacks to the various methods of pollution control, as you probably know if you have recently purchased a car. Prices rise, and in some cases, short-run economic efficiency may be sacrificed.

Still, why shouldn't producers—and, ultimately, the consumers of steel, chemicals, or paper (or any product from a high-pollution industry)—assume the full costs of production, even the pollution clean-up costs? If we are truly concerned about minimizing the degradation of our environment (including not only the visible pollution but also the invisible poisons, such as pesticides, radioactive materials, mercury, etc.), then perhaps we ought to act now, not for ourselves so much as for future generations. Paying the extra price in the short run may well turn out to be a good investment in the long run.

The Household Sector

The other major sector in our economy is the **household sector.** If the business sector organizes resources and supplies goods and services, what economic role does the household sector play?

Households are in a pivotal position in our economy. On the one hand, they supply resources to businesses (land, labor, capital, management); on the other hand, they are consumers of goods and services. About 100 million household units purchase roughly two thirds of the total U.S. economic output each year. In what form do households receive their income?

Looking at national averages, we find that approximately three quarters of the national income flowing to resource suppliers is in the form of wages and salaries. Interest represents about 10 percent of the total, corporate profits and proprietorship incomes are roughly 8 percent each, and rent income makes up the remainder.

Once the money is in our pocketbooks, what do we do with it? Americans spend about 80 percent of their income, and personal taxes take approximately 15 percent. The remaining amount, roughly 5 percent, is saved. (Americans are not known to be great savers!) On the average, households spend about 54 percent of their money on *services* (household operations, financial services, health, transportation, education, recreation, restaurant services, etc.); 32 percent on *nondurable goods* (food, clothing, gasoline, etc.); and only about 14 percent on *durable goods* (anything such as cars, cameras, stoves, VCR's, etc. with a useful life of over a year). Columnist George Will vividly reminds us that there has been a dramatic shift away from durable goods, which, over the years, has brought about a fundamental change in American industry:

> . . . golden arches, not blast furnaces, are becoming the symbols of American enterprise. Today McDonald's has more employees than U.S. Steel. This "once great industrial giant" used to make big locomotives, big Buicks. Now it makes Big Macs.[12]

Then why are services such a large part of the average family budget today? Part of the answer is that it takes more and more repair and maintenance services (and more skilled individuals) to match the quantity and complexity of the durable goods and components of modern housing and transportation. More important, perhaps, is the great increase in the cost of professional services (medical, dental, educational, legal, etc.). The prices of durable goods, on the other hand, have been rising relatively modestly; in fact, some durable product prices (on radios, televisions, VCR's, computers, pocket calculators) have even gone *down* in the past couple of decades. Service costs, in turn, have increased mainly because of relatively low productivity. Let's look at this idea a little more closely.

Productivity is how economists measure the *useful output gained over a standard amount of input* (such as an hour of a worker's time). For example, a 60-word-per-minute typist is twice as productive as a 30-word-per-minute typist. Let's assume that a decade ago a factory employed 50 people and turned out 100 radios a day. By utilizing laborsaving technology, that same factory today might produce 500 radios with only 10 people, demonstrating a dramatic increase in worker productivity. Why did the factory mechanize? It was forced to do so to offset the higher and higher costs of labor. In addition, it was able to mechanize without great difficulty because it is relatively easy to adapt technology to an assembly-line operation. Such mechanization helps to keep product prices lower than they would be without it.

Now consider Helen, the fourth-grade school teacher. Helen provides an important service to society, but she finds it very difficult to increase her productivity. There she stands, in front of her class of 28 students, as her grandmother did (in a one-room schoolhouse) 50 years before her, but Helen feels the school board must increase her salary to match inflation and higher wages throughout the economy. As long as wages continue to rise but productivity remains relatively low or unchanged, households must pay proportionately more for schooling, medical and dental care, government operation, and other services.[13] Some economists feel that without substantial increases in productivity, it will be very difficult to eliminate inflation in our current economic environment, particularly in the service industries. (There are, of course, other factors that contribute to inflation, which will be examined in detail in Chapters 8 and 9.)

Another observation can be made about households. Look around you. You will note with some interest (or perhaps some resentment) that some households receive very large incomes and others receive relatively small incomes. Why are some wages high and others low? One important explanation comes from our old friends *supply* and *demand.*

Both supply and demand must work for us if we are to enjoy high wages. This means that the supply of people with your particular skill must be low and the demand for your skill must be relatively high. High salaries for doctors, for example, are not so much a matter of great skill or life-saving capability as they are a result of a relatively low supply of doctors and the high demand for medical services. If there were millions and millions of doctors in the United States, their average wage could conceivably fall below that of a skilled automobile mechanic. In fact, back in the 1930s, the American Medical Association fought hard to keep the supply of medical practitioners low, realizing that an oversupply might depress wages. The United States continues to have regional shortages of medical personnel, partly because of similar restrictive policies. Other professional groups have also reduced entry into their fields by requiring licensing and certification.[14]

In summary, if we are focusing only on the financial benefit of the household, the lesson should be clear: "Seek an occupation with few practitioners in a market of high demand, and woe unto them who by accident or design find themselves in a market of low demand with a large supply of skilled applicants." What is your occupation or planned occupation? And how do you think supply and demand will affect the market for you?

The discussion of incomes resulting from the supply-demand situation in the resource markets leads us to our final, and perhaps most significant, observation about households in a capitalist society. Recall (from Chapter 1) the basic economic question, "How does the economic system distribute the available output?" We are now able to answer that question. Output goes to those individuals and families who have sufficient incomes from the resource market to generate effective demand in the goods and services markets. If you do not have the opportunity to earn a decent income, you will not have the dollar votes in the product markets. Supply is forthcoming only if there is effective demand, or purchasing power.

A major problem arises, of course, when economic needs and purchasing power are not even remotely in balance. For example, a family might have a critical need for nutritious food (they may even be starving), but if they cannot generate effective demand (because of lack of income), no supply will be forthcoming to these individuals. An exaggerated (but real) example of this occurred during the Great Depression in the 1930s, when people went hungry while farmers plowed under perfectly nutritious food; there was insufficient income to purchase food and, therefore, insufficient demand to make it profitable to produce food. Poor people in the United States and in the less-developed countries of the world face the same situation today.

On the other hand, we might find (even during a depression) a wealthy family feeding their dogs steak every day, because the income is there and the purchasing power is there—and the economic system responds to these factors. Thus, the **second tragic flaw of capitalism** is its tendency to be unresponsive in the absence of effective demand, no matter what the basic need may be.

What can be done about such critical flaws in our economic system? How does our basically capitalist economy resolve the conflicts posed by increasing industrial pollution and a lack of purchasing power for the poor?

We deal with them primarily through government action. Government, then, is the third major sector in our economy. In a sense, government takes over when private-enterprise capitalism fails to deal with fundamental economic problems. Government is a large sector and exerts tremendous influence in economic affairs. It's time we took a closer look at its function and operation.

Questions for Thought and Discussion

1. Do you believe that it might be possible to correct the first tragic flaw of capitalism without government intervention? Why or why not?

2. What would happen to the circular flow of our economic system if consumers began saving large percentages of their incomes?

3. Although service industries employ roughly 75 percent of working Americans, service output is about 50 percent of the total output. Explain why the two figures are not the same. What might likely be a future trend in these two statistics?

4. What would the world be like if the law of diminishing returns did not apply when a variable input, such as labor, was applied to a fixed input, such as land or capital?

NEW PERSPECTIVES

Looking Deeply . . .

In a brief, but intriguing essay entitled "Interbeing,"* Buddhist writer Thich Nhat Hanh asks us to "look deeply" at a page of writing and reflect upon what we "see" in the paper.

Having learned some basic economics, you probably can "see" a paper, ink, and a publishing company making profits and trying to satisfy their investors. Can you "see" a useful product on the one hand, but also some pollution (First Tragic Flaw) and deforestation on the other hand? Undoubtedly you will also be able to visualize a tree—perhaps an aspen, as it is often the species used in pulp and paper manufacturing. Hanh, however, goes a step further; he asks us to see the logger who

> . . . cut the tree and brought it to the mill . . . and we see wheat. We know that the logger cannot exist without his daily bread.

If we continue to "look deeply," Hanh suggests that we can also "see sunshine" or a cloud:

> Without a cloud, there will be no rain; without rain, the trees cannot grow.

Eventually, Hanh's journey takes us into an ever expanding, interconnected universe of widely diverse ecological factors:

> . . . time, space, the earth, the rain, the minerals in the soil, the sunshine, the cloud, the river . . .

and so on.

And finally, as we read a page of someone's writing, Hanh insists that we should be able to "see our own perceptions" as well:

> Your mind is here and mine is also . . .

Question: Take 20 minutes to slowly and thoughtfully go through as many economic and ecological factors that went into this page of text.

Question: What about the last automobile you were in? "Look deeply" into its raw materials, manufacture, its ultimate use (and misuse), etc. Are there any applications of the tragic flaws? Again, take your time. Be thoughtful.

*Thich Nhat Hanh. *Peace is Every Step*. New York: Bantam Books, 1991.

5

Government

Why do we have government? I once met a man who stated quite emphatically that society would be better off with no government whatsoever, except for police protection and national defense. "Government is basically evil," he said. "It's not only very costly and ineffective, but every government action subtracts from individual freedom." He concluded that everything the government is doing now could be better accomplished by an unregulated free-enterprise market system. So once more: "Why do we have government? What's it doing for us?"

Tragic Flaws

Indeed, we have already started to build a case for government activity, beginning with the circular flowchart in Figure 4-1. For example, without government, who would provide for (and regulate) the money supply? We have seen that money is essential to the operation of our complex economy; in addition, the amount of money in circulation must be carefully adjusted to changing economic conditions. Also recall our discussion of the two tragic flaws of capitalism. Addressing the first flaw, how would our present private-enterprise system halt pollution and environmental degradation without government intervention? How could we stop businesses from using the air and water as free garbage cans to lower their production costs? Self-regulation does not work very well, nor will it work as long as pollution-prone industries feel pressured to minimize costs and maximize profits. There seems to be only one realistic solution to this problem. The government must step in to force producers to pay the full costs of production, including pollution control.

In many cases, the pollution problem cannot be solved on the local level alone. There are two reasons for this. First, the *neighborhood effects* of polluted water (or air) often extend beyond the confines of a specific locality. A river does not recognize municipal or state boundaries. As an illustration, if some company pollutes the Mississippi River in Minneapolis, it will affect residents not only in Moline, Illinois, but also farther downriver in St. Louis, Missouri, and New Orleans, Louisiana. Air pollution too affects neighboring and even distant regions.

Second, national pollution laws are necessary to prevent polluters from shutting down their operations in a state that has strict controls and moving them to a state that is more lenient. State governments might hesitate to stop polluters if it meant throwing local residents out of work.

Carrying this point one step further, what about international pollution? Shouldn't there be worldwide laws (and provisions for their enforcement) to prevent the pollution of the global oceans and atmosphere? We have already seen some of the severe consequences of international pollution, including the incidence of radiation drift from a Soviet Union nuclear reactor accident in 1986. Also consider the continuing environmental problems of acid rain, the greenhouse effect, and the depletion of the upper ozone layer of our atmosphere. If we apply the logic of neighborhood effects on a global scale, we must conclude that, in certain cases, international laws will be necessary.

According to some observers, the question we should be asking is not so much do we need controls but will we be able to control worldwide pollution in time? Indeed, there is growing evidence that the oceans are generally becoming less habitable for marine life. Industrial pollution, garbage, and invisible poisons have been detected in almost every major ocean zone. In addition, some scientists predict the eventual extinction of a wide variety of life forms if present pollution and tropical deforestation trends continue. There is a growing awareness that the problem of worldwide pollution cannot be solved by the market system on its own. Government action—supported by people attuned to the dictum "think globally, act locally"—may just become the critical component of our quality of life as we approach a new century.*

The second basic flaw of capitalism is its inability to meet fundamental human needs in the absence of effective demand. So many families and individuals in our society, for one reason or another, do not or cannot earn sufficient incomes to purchase the minimum necessities of life. Some are too old, others are disabled, and many are children. Some are unskilled and can't find work; the skills of many others are no longer in demand. We need to ask ourselves, "What obligations do we, as a comparatively wealthy society, have to these people?" Few would want to see them go hungry or be without shelter or minimum health care.

Consider, too, the question of social stability. In his critique of "Reaganomics" (which made large cuts in social programs but reduced tax rates for upper-income groups), historian Arthur Schlesinger, Jr., argued that our government's sensitivity to people in need has helped maintain capitalism's amazing continuity:

> Capitalism has survived because of a continuing and remarkably successful effort to humanize the industrial order, to cushion the operations of the economic system, to combine pecuniary opportunity with social cohesion. It has survived because of a long campaign, mounted by liberals, to reduce the suffering—and thereby the resentment and rebelliousness—of those to whom the accidents of birth deny an equal chance.[15]

Income redistribution comes in all kinds of packages: welfare and public health programs, Medicare, etc. Although there is general agreement that the government should play some role in income redistribution, there is much argument over *how much* public subsidy should be made available to the poor. Indeed, few subjects in economics generate such a heated and

---

*A more detailed discussion of atmospheric pollution and possible climate change appears in Chapter 12.

bitter debate. Some have suggested that income be redistributed in the form of government jobs or even a guaranteed minimum income. But should this subsidy be maintained at a bare survival level, or should enough money be distributed to provide needy families with a moderate standard of living? We will examine this subject further in Chapter 6.

We also need government to help maintain competition. Even the most bitter opponent of government practices can appreciate the value of some type of antitrust legislation. Capitalism, left on its own, has often produced an increasing concentration of economic power, as large and powerful firms eliminated rivals by fair (or foul) means. As proof, we have only to look at the pre-antitrust days of the late nineteenth century. It was an age when gigantic trusts fixed prices and monopolized manufacturing and commerce, with little regard for overall economic efficiency or the interest of the consumer. It may seem ironic that we need strong public intervention to guarantee the survival of our private competitive capitalist system, but most economists feel that we do.

Public Goods

Without government, who would provide us with our **public goods?** Public goods are essential to the welfare of society, yet they are either too cumbersome or unprofitable to be supplied to consumers by private industries. A road is a good example. It's doubtful that you would ever consider building a highway. Even if you could afford it, why would you personally make such a large investment when a lot of other people would also be using the road—at your expense? Nor would we expect General Motors or Ford to build millions of miles of roads, or doctors to finance hospitals, or campers to totally subsidize national, state, and local parks.

What about libraries, parks and wilderness areas, police and fire protection, public radio and television, plus the thousands of local schools and universities in our country? These are all public goods, and if everyone is to enjoy them, we need to generate demand for these goods and services through a system of taxation and public expenditure. Without a social commitment to financing public goods, these necessities of a civilized society would be available only to the relatively wealthy.

Without government, who would play the role of economic **umpire** to enforce the so-called rules of the game? Who would make sure that everyone plays fairly? Someone must define the legal responsibilities of business operations; someone must enforce contracts, and spell out property rights; someone must keep an eye out for misleading advertising, for foods and drugs that might impair the public health, and for unsafe products that could kill or maim thousands of consumers. We can be sure that this someone will probably not step forward from private industry. We know that some businesses, left unregulated, will engage in deceitful advertising or, for example, sell baby cribs in which hundreds of infants could strangle themselves or manufacture dangerous toys. In these and many other situations, we can't expect consumers to always be sufficiently informed to protect themselves and their families.

But how far should government regulation of business go? Where is that line between government as Big Brother and government as legitimate protector? We know, for example, that some people slip and fracture their skulls in their bathtubs each year. Should we require all persons to wear safety helmets when they step into the tub? Of course not. But what about requiring children and adults to wear helmets when they ride bicycles or motorcycles? Just how much regulated safety is too much? To what degree should we pursue a philosophy of individual responsibility and let the consumer beware? Taking this issue one step further, when does excessive government protection tend to minimize or circumvent consumers' initiatives to protect themselves?

We should also take a look at the *cost* of consumer protection. For example, would it be wise to require Detroit to build an automobile bumper designed to withstand a crash at 50 miles per hour? Certainly a good idea in theory, but how much more would this "super" bumper cost the consumer? Where do we draw the line?

Unfortunately, the study of economics does not always give clear-cut answers to these questions. Economists, with their tools of analysis, can help to determine the economic costs and benefits of different actions and policies. In the end, however, such decisions are usually made by lawmakers and regulatory agencies that attempt to strike a political balance between the interests of businesses, consumers, and taxpayers.

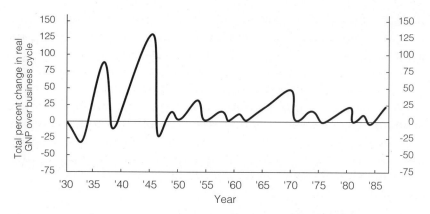

FIGURE 5-1   The severity of economic swings in U.S. business cycles has been reduced since World War II, partly due to government intervention. A variety of stabilization policies are related to taxes, expenditures, and periodic adjustments in the money supply and interest rate. (Graph concept: R. J. Eggert.)

The Business Cycle

Finally, in our quest to explore government's role, we might take a moment to consider Figure 5-1. First of all, note that the heavy line is an approximate indicator of what economists call the **business cycle,***—the large (and sometimes not so large) swings in business activity over time. Note especially the downward trends—from the cycle's peaks to its troughs, or low points.

These downward movements represent times of special economic hardship, including periods of higher than average unemployment, bankruptcies, and underutilization of resources. Indeed, we learned the hard lesson during the Great Depression of the 1930s that unregulated capitalism does not always have an automatic mechanism to pull the economy out of a severe slump. Also, during periods of extremely high economic activity, we may be confronted with a problem on the other side of the business cycle—unacceptable inflation such as we experienced

*For a superb discussion on business cycles—how they start, how they are measured, how they end—see Alfred Malabre's *Understanding the New Economy* (Dow Jones—Irwin, 1989), particularly Chapter 5, "Ups and Downs."

toward the end of the 1970s. It is the existence of these large swings in the economy's business cycle and the accompanying problems that we will now call the **third tragic flaw of capitalism.**

In times of economic slumps and high inflation, the government is pressured to take initiatives to help smooth out the severe swings in the business cycle. Note in Figure 5-1 that although the cycle has not been eliminated, each of its exaggerated parts has, since World War II, been leveled out somewhat (and its duration has been shortened)—primarily through government budgetary and monetary policies (more on these policies in Chapters 8 and 9).

In summary, then, the business cycle forces government to become an active defender of the nation's economic health. Like the white knight in the fairy tale, government intervention attempts to slay the double-headed dragon of depression and inflation and to generally smooth out the business cycle.

Yet as successfully as government solves problems in some areas of the economy, our white knight can also have an unpleasant side. We know that some government activity is badly planned, expensive, and (at times) downright harmful. We can cite numerous examples of overregulation and needless meddling in affairs that are none of the government's business.

We have also seen certain safety laws enacted that are good in theory but, when the fine print is read, turn out to be unrealistic impediments to the operation of legitimate small businesses. We have seen some bad effects from restrictive zoning and outmoded building codes, as well as unnecessary harassment from inspectors, all of which may stifle innovation and initiative. We have seen government-sponsored urban renewal programs disembowel neighborhoods and build poorly planned public-housing highrises in their place. And, finally, we have seen how meddlesome the government's bureaucracy can be, or noted the chilling effects of centralized data banks and government intelligence—an insidious world of phone taps and computer retrieval systems where a sense of privacy may sometimes be destroyed. No, not all government action is good.

But certainly some government regulation is essential in a complex society. If government destroys some freedoms, it enhances others. Although it does so imperfectly at times, government subsidizes education for everyone, creates employment in times of recession, enforces equal employment rights, and tries to evolve policies to deal with severe and pervasive national problems such as drugs, AIDS, child abuse, crime, and homeless-ness. Government also builds clinics and public parks, supports agricultural research, and looks after the environment. It finances countless programs that try to help people who need help. Without government intervention, our complex economy would have a difficult time surviving.

The ambivalence of big government—combining both the good and the bad (and often not being able to tell the difference)—sometimes creates an identity problem for this benevolent titan. Perhaps no one captured this sense of ambivalence better than Associated Press writer Saul Pett, when he likened our federal government to a

> . . . big, bumbling, generous, naive, inquisitive, acquisitive, intrusive, meddlesome giant . . . with a heart of gold and holes in his pockets, an incredible hulk, a "10-ton marshmallow" lumbering along an uncertain road of good intentions somewhere between capitalism and socialism, an implausible giant who fights wars, sends men to the moon, explores the ends of the universe, feeds the hungry, heals the sick, helps the helpless, a thumping complex of guilt trying mightily to make up for past sins to the satisfaction of nobody. . . a malleable vulnerable colossus pulled every which way by everybody who wants a piece of him, which is everybody.[16]

We can thus recognize the tremendous pressure on government to intervene in the private economy: to regulate, to provide public goods and services, to subsidize, to redistribute income, and at times to stabilize the business cycle. Although it would be difficult to determine precisely, economists have estimated that roughly one quarter to one third of all U.S. economic activity is strongly influenced by public or government decisions. Indeed, the economic reality of our system is a far cry from the pure capitalist model, in which the means of production and control over resources would be strictly in private hands. We therefore say that our economic system is not pure capitalism but **mixed capitalism**—mixed with a large dose of government financed by taxes.

It is perhaps time to take a closer look at the details of these taxes and expenditures. Indeed, there are so many different sources of government revenue and areas of expenditure (federal, state, and local), it's no wonder the average voter-taxpayer is bewildered. So where do we start?

Taxes and Expenditures

Let's begin with the broad flows of government finance on the federal level. The largest single source of federal income is the **personal income tax** that many of us dread when the middle of April rolls around each year. In fact, almost one half of all federal revenue comes from this tax. The second largest tax, contributing about one third of all federal tax receipts, is the **payroll tax** (Social Security). The **corporate income tax** is third in importance. **Excise taxes** (a tax on a specific item like cigarettes), **customs duties,** and **estate taxes** make up the remainder.

Where does the federal government spend our tax money? The largest single area (approximately 50 percent) is in the form of domestic social expenditures, including Social Security, health, education, veterans' benefits and other forms of income security. It's important to note that over half of these benefits are earmarked for retirees (mainly Social Security and Medicare). Due to growing numbers and effective lobbying, the elderly have gained a steadily increasing proportion of federal income disbursements or *entitlements* during the 1970s and 80s. As defense expenditures—the second largest category of spending—shrink because of the dissolution of the Soviet Union, the elderly's proportion is likely to get larger and more controversial.*

At the state level, we find that, on average, the **sales tax** contributes roughly one half of the revenue; the other half is derived from personal and corporate income taxes plus licenses, permits, and fees. The states spend over one quarter of this revenue on education, with public welfare coming in a close second. Health, highways, and public safety follow in overall importance.

---

* See, for example, Lee Smith's article, "The Tyranny of America's Old." (*Fortune,* Jan. 13, 1992, p. 68.)

The local tax scene is dramatically different. Local governments derive almost all their revenues from the **property tax.** Education takes more than 40 percent of this money. Welfare, health, housing, and public safety (police and fire) follow in diminishing importance. The total amount of federal, state, and local taxes spent on publicly supported education is a very large sum indeed.

Tax Philosophies

What are the basic differences between the taxes we pay? We generally categorize a tax as either a benefits-received tax or an ability-to-pay tax. The philosophy of **benefits-received taxation** is that "The person who pays the tax ought to get the benefits from the expenditure of that tax." Perhaps the best illustration of this is gasoline tax revenue, which is specifically earmarked for highway construction and maintenance. Hunting license fees, tuition for state universities, and airport tax (to pay for anti-hijacking security) are other examples. In each case, the money from the tax is earmarked and funneled back into a direct service for the taxpayer. To many people, the benefits-received approach seems to be the fairest possible taxation system. But if this is true, then why don't we base all our taxes on this principle?

If we applied only the benefits-received principle, there would be some major problems. For example, how would we pay for national defense? Would everyone—rich and poor alike—pay the same dollar amount? That would hardly be practical. How would we finance public schools on a benefits-received principle? Would we only tax families with children (the larger the family, the greater the tax)? How could we guarantee that everyone received an equal opportunity to pursue an education? We couldn't. For this reason, and others, we have some taxes based on the **ability-to-pay principle,** which do not penalize lower-income groups or deprive them of the various benefits of government expenditures.

More specifically, the ability-to-pay philosophy says, "Those people who have more financial resources (income and wealth) should pay more tax." Many economists feel that the best example of this kind of tax is the **progressive income tax.** A progressive tax means the greater your income, *the greater the percentage of tax you pay.*

A simplified progressive income tax became law with the Tax Reform act of 1986—modified again in 1990. The elimination of many loopholes made it possible to lower the maximum bracket rate from 50 to 31 percent. Combined with the intermediate brackets of 15 and 28 percent, Congress continued the progressive philosophy but reduced the number of brackets compared to the pre-1986 system.

There are also **regressive taxes.** If a purely progressive tax is a good example of ability-to-pay, a regressive tax is a good example of the opposite situation. With a regressive tax, *the poor pay a higher percentage of their income* in taxes than the wealthy do. A good example is a $1 park-entrance fee. Obviously, $1 is a larger percentage of a poor person's income than of a rich person's income. Also, tuition can sometimes be considered regressive, as can the property tax. For example, a home-owning retired couple may easily find themselves paying a sizable percentage of their relatively small income as property tax.

The sales tax might also be considered an example of a regressive tax, since poor families usually pay tax on all their income (because all or nearly all of it is usually spent). The wealthy save or invest much of their income, so that a sizable portion of it is not exposed to the sales tax. Thus, looking at total incomes, the poor wind up paying a higher percentage as sales tax. A number of states have minimized the regressiveness of their sales tax by exempting some necessary items, such as food and prescription medicines.

Generally, most economists feel that a simplified progressive income tax is a fairer way to raise government revenue than sales or property taxes. Of course, any method of taxing away spending power from the public is going to be unpopular. Taxpayer hostility can often be traced to objections to specific public expenditures. The one expenditure that is perhaps the most controversial is welfare. Let's take a closer look at this issue, as well as at the broader problem of poverty in the United States.

Questions for Thought and Discussion

1. If Big Brother was not here in 1984 (as George Orwell's novel predicted), when will he be here? Is he already here? Explain.

2. Should local public schools be financed primarily by property taxes? Why or why not? Also, should college tuition be based upon the ability-to-pay principle? Again, defend your position.

3. How important are property taxes to your local community? Are they collected at the state level, county level, or city level? What is the resulting tax revenue used to buy?

4. Public goods are consumed in equal amounts by the public. Comment.

5. Are gambling revenues a good method to finance government budgets? What kind of "tax" are they? If applicable research the use of gambling in your state.

NEW PERSPECTIVES

Government as Umpire . . . You Make the Call!

As with an official football game, "government as umpire" is never an easy job! The goal, among other things, is to enforce economic fair play, protect the innocent and unwary, and at times, become a watchdog over commercial activities that grossly violate society's values. Yet all too often, the "correct" viewpoint is not always clear. Take the case of beer ads.

Under the Bush administration, the Surgeon General (Antonia Novello) tried to pressure the beer companies to change the content of their TV commercials. Not surprisingly, the beer industry thought it was none of the government's business. Take a moment to look at some of the arguments; as you do, consider not only the specific issue of beer commercials but also the broader role of government regulation itself.

First, Ms. Novello, as part of her strategy to combat underage drinking, was quoted as saying,

> I must call for industry's voluntary elimination of the types of alcohol advertising that appeal to youth on the basis of certain lifestyle appeals, sexual appeal, sports appeal, or risky activities, as well as advertising with the more blatant youth appeals of cartoon characters and youth slang.

As expected, the beer industry called her appeal "an attempt at censorship." More specifically, James Sanders of the Beer Institute said,

> I just don't think anyone is going to jump forth and concede that the surgeon general has either the right or power to decide what is acceptable or unacceptable for the American people to watch.

In addition a spokesman for Anheuser-Busch claimed that his company's commercials did not really increase overall beer consumption, but simply reshuffled existing beer consumers toward their (Budweiser) products:

> We think that the posse is out and has the noose around an innocent victim here. Advertising is just not a significant factor in really making anybody drink . . . what it is successful in doing is getting the drinker to drink *our* products.

Question: First, is it the government's business to suggest these kinds of changes? Based on your own observations or experience, are the beer industry arguments convincing? Specifically, on the beer-ad issue, how would you make the call.

Question: Can your class research and evaluate a different "umpire" topic? Possibilities include toy or automobile safety, food quality regulation, environmental laws, workplace safety rules, etc. If possible, organize a class debate where two groups take different stands while a third acts as umpire or jury.

All quotes taken from "Surgeon General Wants to Age Alcohol Ads," by Hilary Scott, *The Wall Street Journal,* November 5, 1991: p. B1.

6

Poverty

The following portion of a letter to the editor of a newspaper in St. Paul, Minnesota, describes the writer's feelings about people who receive public assistance:

> . . . according to a newspaper item, one AFDC [Aid to Families with Dependent Children] recipient said, "We are people too." Yes, they "are people too," people who are unwilling to go to work to support themselves and their children as long as they are able to steal from the rest of us who have worked hard and long for many years. . . . What about the rest of us who have worked all of our lives and now find ourselves "short of money" too, because we have to share with these people our hard-earned money? Where do they think we get our money?

It's certainly an honest letter. It expresses considerable anger, and frustration too. But it's also, it seems, a somewhat misleading letter, because the writer appears to be blaming all those who are poor for creating their own poverty. There are, in fact, more than 30 million men, women, and children (mostly children) who are unable to successfully participate in and benefit from our economic system. For one reason or another, they simply do not earn adequate incomes to buy the necessities of life.

Still, research indicates that most adults do want to work and will work, given the chance. For example, in 50 percent of

all poverty families, at least one member of the household holds a job; in 20 percent of all poverty families, both parents are working.[17] Working families often remain poor because wages are too low. If, for example, a person worked full time, 40 hours a week, 52 weeks a year at the federal minimum wage, that person's yearly income would still fall significantly below the income definition of poverty in the United States for an urban family of four!

The writer of the opening letter was apparently not aware of some other statistics related to our welfare programs. The federal government reports that, on national average, most welfare recipients are children. (Today, one out of every five American children under six years of age lives in poverty.) The second largest category includes the blind, aged, and disabled. Mothers of poverty children are third; able-bodied fathers, fourth.

The widespread belief "Once on welfare, always on welfare" is another of the many misconceptions about our welfare programs. Examining national averages, 50 percent of poverty families are considered temporarily poor; they have been on welfare only one or two years out of the ten years studied. One in six poverty families are persistently poor; they have been receiving welfare for more than eight years. In most cases, poverty families mix work and welfare with assistance when needed, especially in times of family break-ups, unemployment, disability, or serious illness.[18]

Another commonly stated belief is "Welfare's getting most of our tax money." Out of all federal expenditures in the early 1990s, federal income payments to the poor were a distant fourth in overall importance—after (1) programs for the elderly (Social Security and Medicare), (2) defense, and (3) interest on the public debt. In many states, assistance payments to the poor are so low they do not even meet the state's own definition of poverty.

Of course, there are the infuriating cases of people who, through welfare fraud, live high off the hog, buying expensive electronic gadgets, new cars, or other items that average, hardworking, taxpaying families feel they cannot afford. These are the cases that make the headlines; critics jump on them, and they become the grist for resentful gossip. From a broad statistical point of view, such criticism is generally undeserved. Most poor families, given a choice, don't want handouts; they need income assistance to get through short- to medium-term family and financial crises. In short, our poor need a level of understanding from those of us who aren't doing so badly—not misconceptions based on prejudice or sentimentality but a true understanding of the realities of poverty in the United States.

What are these realities? From a historical point of view, one of the classics on this subject is Michael Harrington's *The Other America*. Although Harrington's statistics are dated (the book was originally published in the early 1960s), many feel that his observations are still surprisingly true in the 1990s. More specifically, what are the characteristics of the "other America"?

First of all, the poor are invisible. Except for the urban homeless, most poor people live off the beaten track. We do not normally encounter these pockets of poverty, whether they occur in deep southern rural areas, black or hispanic ghettos, or even the American suburbs.[19]

What is even more important, however, is that the poor are politically invisible, making them vulnerable to shifts in national sentiment and often powerless to initiate programs to defend themselves within the political arena:

> . . . the poor are politically invisible. . . . The people of the other America do not, by far and large, belong to unions, to fraternal organizations, or to political parties. They are without lobbies of their own; they put forward no legislative program. As a group, they are atomized. They have no face; they have no voice.[20]

Poverty Groups

The poor also belong to different subgroups that share the common problem of low income but have their own special difficulties. There are, for example, the **aged.** Although their poverty percentage has come down over the years (due mainly to inflation-adjusted Social Security and Medicare), more than 10 percent of this group still falls below the poverty line. Especially vulnerable are widowed women over 65 years of age; their poverty percentages are much higher than the national averages. A black retired woman living alone has, for example, nearly a 50 percent chance of living below the poverty line.

Another poverty group is the **structurally unemployed.** The people in this group, even though they have skills and even though the economy may be booming, still find themselves without work. This can happen, for example, when employment opportunities disappear because of a fundamental change in technology, global competition, or a major shift in consumer demand. Such structural changes in the economy often leave pockets of poverty that can continue for years and years. The structurally unemployed include the underground coal miners in Kentucky and West Virginia and the iron-ore workers in northern Michigan and Minnesota who watched their livelihoods dissolve as the mines closed down temporarily or, more often than not, permanently. This group also includes the New England textile workers whose jobs were exported to low-paid Italians, Mexicans, and Taiwanese, as well as the autoworkers and steelworkers whose factories have been closing down as large-scale manufacturing modernizes or trims down or as the nation itself slowly changes from durable-goods industries to services and high-technology production.

Other poverty groups include the migrant workers of the fruit- and vegetable-producing states, the marginal farmers and sharecroppers of the deep South, and the millions living in the black and Spanish-speaking slums of our northeastern cities. And since *The Other America* was published in 1962, we've witnessed a surprisingly large increase in the poverty of **single-parent households,** 90 percent of which are headed by the mother. The rise of unwed motherhood and divorce, combined with little or no financial commitment from the fathers (more than 50 percent of these families, for example, receive no child-care support), has created the most significant change in poverty statistics in the past couple of decades—what is sometimes referred to as the **feminization of poverty.*** Adding to the female poverty problem is the trend for women to work in relatively low-paying jobs with little or no benefits, and also the demographic dilemma of older women facing years of widowhood with meager retirement income.

And, finally, another recent poverty group also on the increase is simply called the **underclass.** The people of this group are essentially uprooted and frequently homeless. Although many are living on the streets of large American cities, their precise numbers are unknown because they exist outside the regular social-services network. They include drug addicts, the rural unemployed, undocumented aliens, teenage runaways, and nonviolent mental patients who have been deinstitutionalized

---

* A term coined by Diana M. Pearce, director of Catholic University's Center for National Policy Review.

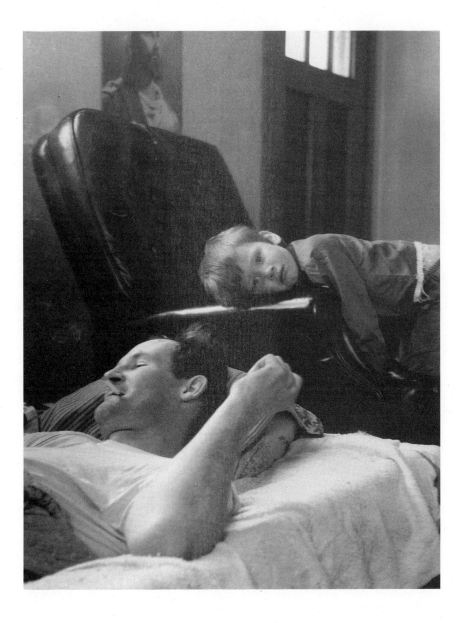

but given insufficient economic resources to purchase or rent shelter.[21] The American underclass provides us with vivid evidence of capitalism's second tragic flaw—its inability to meet the basic economic needs of its poorest and most vulnerable class of citizens.

The reality of poverty includes some individuals who were simply born with the "wrong" set of parents, with the "wrong" color skin, or in the "wrong" part of the country—born into a kind of *vicious circle*. The average beginning incomes of nonwhites, for example, are roughly 60 percent those of whites. As for education, more than twice as many whites finish high school as nonwhites do. All the way down the list, whites enjoy clear-cut advantages in every economic category. One out of every two whites has a white-collar occupation, compared with one in three nonwhites. Unemployment is at least double for nonwhites in all age groups, and nonwhite unemployment among young college graduates is more than triple that of whites. When we examine the unemployment statistics for minority teenagers, we discover that between 25 and 30 percent of all nonwhite teenagers are actively searching for employment but can't find jobs! Indeed, this may be America's most profound economic tragedy—that a sizable group of young men and women are not given the opportunity to become integrated into the mainstream of society with an entry-level job.

This vicious economic circle can be viewed as a kind of sickness, with the cure often out of the patient's control. Communities with low incomes, for example, may very well have substandard schools, staffed either with young, inexperienced teachers (at the lowest end of the salary scale) or uninspired teachers who are not good enough to move on (even though they would like to). Lacking good models of middle-class mobility and economic success, young people receive little inspiration or encouragement and tend to drop out more frequently than middle-class students. Students coming out of a low-expectation environment with few, if any, marketable skills, wind up with the economy's most menial, dead-end, lowest-paying jobs (or no jobs at all)—and the economic circle of poverty begins all over again. You can start anywhere in this circle and eventually wind up in the same place.

There are other factors to consider as well, such as racial and sexual discrimination, mental and physical handicaps, chronic drug dependence, poor health, and the very real fear of living and raising children in high crime neighborhoods. Even in the purchase of necessities, such as food, transportation, and shelter, poor families find it difficult to be efficient consumers. For example, food is often bought in smaller quantities, but at higher

prices per unit weight. Lower-income housing is frequently not energy-efficient, making it more expensive to keep warm in the winter or cool in the summer. Each additional factor makes it more and more difficult to break out of the poverty circle.

Of course, there have been numerous successful breakaways —individuals who have triumphed over the poverty environment with intelligence, hard work, good luck, and, frequently, good connections. They are now highly skilled tradespeople, wealthy businessmen and women, bank presidents, court justices, mayors, and college professors. But like the welfare myths (the ten-children families living it up with expensive food and driving Cadillacs), people who have beaten poverty are the exceptions, the statistical aberrations. The truth is that the vicious circle of poverty is just that—and to make headway against its odds, you usually need help.

Government Assistance

But what kind of help? Henry David Thoreau once said, "If I knew for a certainty that a man was coming to my house with the conscious design of doing me good, I should run for my life—for fear that I should get some of his good done to me." [22] Most poor people would probably agree with Thoreau's distaste for the overbearing do-gooder. The poor often resent the battalions of government investigators and even the well-intentioned volunteer workers who sometimes may offend in their zeal to help. This is not to say that certain government and private programs have not done some good.

We have to keep in mind, though, that poverty is basically an economic problem; its solution, therefore, must also be economic. In short, the poor need one of two things:

1. help to become economically productive, *or*

2. access to subsidized incomes

When we can guarantee everyone access to educational/ training programs and commensurate job opportunities or a guaranteed minimum income, we will have come a long way toward removing capitalism's basic flaw of need versus demand. But how far have we moved in this direction?

First, let's consider the question of productivity and education. Although everyone has the legal right to a free public education, early schooling for many poor people is more often than not substandard. In many cases, even functional literacy is not guaranteed at the conclusion of 12 years of school. Schools and facilities in poor districts simply must be upgraded, particularly in the basic skills area. Fortunately, many states, prodded by alarming educational reports and growing public concern, are making headway in this area.

Yet to be productive in a modern, changing economy, it is also desirable (even necessary) to go beyond high school. Research shows that high school graduates who continue their education become more productive and earn substantially more than their counterparts who do not.

One economist points out that college students in the mid-1980s received approximately $12,000 of direct or indirect public subsidy and asks why noncollege-bound high-school graduates (and dropouts) cannot have access to a similar subsidy. He suggests offering these individuals "skill vouchers" worth an equivalent amount of subsidy that, in turn, could be used for vocational training.[23] This proposal, along with a steadily growing, job-creating economy (see Chapter 8), could indeed help to upgrade the living standards of people who are currently underproductive.

Other individuals or families will, either intermittently or (in some cases) permanently, need subsidized incomes. What then are our current programs in this area, and equally important, how effective are they? Let's take a look.

Currently, our government helps to subsidize poor people in two ways—with transfer payments and goods and services. Specific programs direct **transfer payments** to certain qualified families. These programs are aimed at the elderly, blind, and disabled (Supplemental Security Income Program) and at children and their mothers (Aid to Families with Dependent Children, or AFDC). Social Security, unemployment compensation, and veterans' benefits are also considered transfer payments, although they are paid to people in all income groups and not just to the poor.

Our government also distributes **goods and services** to the needy in lieu of cash. A prime example of this is the Food Stamp program. Another example is Medical Assistance, or Medicaid, which provides families with medical care at the government's expense. Others are public housing, day care, and rent-supplement programs, as well as the successful federal Head Start program. In larger cities, free medical clinics are also made available to lower-income families. Whether these types of service programs should be "cashed out" and the money supplied directly to these families in place of free goods and services is a subject of debate. If this were done, the families could use the cash to compete for food, housing, and medical care in the free market.

Let's return to transfer payments and take an in-depth look at one of our largest income subsidy programs—welfare. We have already noted that intense resentment is frequently directed toward the beneficiaries of welfare; we have also examined some of the myths surrounding welfare and discovered that many of these opinions are simply not supported by fact. However, we have yet to analyze this program from the standpoint of its economic effectiveness. Is welfare good or bad? Does it help or hinder the poor? Evaluating the program as a whole, most economists feel that the present-day welfare system is less than a complete success. Some feel it is poorly designed, inefficient, and expensive—that it often does more harm than good in its attempts to solve the overall problem of poverty. Let's look at some of the problems.

First, the welfare program does not always satisfy the basic economic needs of the people it is designed to serve. Remember that in many states, the amount of welfare paid does not even meet the state's own definition of poverty. The states come up with a figure that reflects a poverty level of living, and then pay the welfare family anywhere from 30 to 80 percent of that amount.

Next, the welfare system (like many bureaucracies) is frequently inefficient. Study the welfare procedures in your city or county, or visit your local welfare office and talk to the employees. You will probably note that a great deal of money and time are spent on red tape, paperwork, income or means tests, questionnaires, evaluations, and investigations. As a result, valuable resources are not available to directly help the poor.

Welfare can also be dehumanizing. Unsympathetic administrators can be suspicious, demeaning, and condescending to new applicants. Those already on welfare are subjected to inquiries and potential surveillance of their lives. Welfare agencies often reflect the prevailing attitude that to receive public assistance is shameful: "The poor have only themselves to blame." Thus, many deserving poor people are too proud to ask for financial help, even when they need it.

Finally, our present welfare system has the unintended effect of encouraging the breakup of families. In some states, for example, a woman with children is refused aid if her able-bodied husband is still a part of the family, even though he may be unemployed. Financial pressures frequently translate into personal tensions and animosities that often lead to the separation or divorce of parents.

Why have we retained such an inefficient income-subsidy system for so long? We tolerate it partly because welfare does have its advantages. Welfare does allow children to stay with their mothers, and it does add something to the meager incomes of the aged and disabled. In addition, it has paid for health services and nursing care when they were critically needed. Furthermore, billion-dollar bureaucracies, no matter how inefficient or ineffective they may be, have an uncanny knack for survival within the political system. But surely there must be a better way to deliver financial assistance to millions of poor

Americans without the drawbacks we have outlined here. Some economists feel that, in fact, there is a more efficient method: it's called the **negative income tax.**

The Negative Income Tax

The idea of a negative income tax originated with Milton Friedman, a conservative economist and an influential maverick of the economics profession. Friedman has long advocated policies that adhere to a fundamental criterion: the enhancement of personal economic freedom and choice. In general, he believes that a decentralized market system will best meet this objective, although it won't necessarily alleviate poverty. Friedman first outlined his alternative to our present welfare system in his book *Capitalism and Freedom;* since the early 1960s, the concept of a negative income tax has gained wide respect.

To understand Friedman's ideas, let's look at the income situations of the Smith, Jones, and Baker families. We will assume that Smith has the largest annual income of $14,000; next comes Jones with $12,000 and, finally, Baker with $9,000:

SMITH	JONES	BAKER
$14,000	$12,000	$9,000

What amount of federal income tax will each of these three families pay? Let's review the procedure for determining income tax, using the Smith family as an example.

Smith will not pay tax on his entire income of $14,000 because all taxpayers are allowed to subtract certain exemptions and deductions from their gross income. For simplicity's sake, let's say that the tax exemption for each dependent (including Smith, the head of the household) is $2,000. Thus, for a family of four, the total exemption (what Smith can subtract from his gross income) is $8,000 ($2,000 × 4).

All taxpayers are also allowed to take specific deductions. Although middle- and higher-income families sometimes itemize, a standard deduction is usually taken by lower-income families.

Smith has $8,000 in exemptions. If we assume that he can also take a standard deduction of $4,000, then the combined total exemptions and deductions for the Smith family will be $12,000:

Exemptions	$8,000
Standard deduction	4,000
Total	$12,000

Thus, instead of paying tax on his total $14,000 income, Smith is allowed to subtract exemptions and deductions of $12,000. His **taxable income** will therefore be only $2,000. The lowest tax rate is 15 percent, so Smith will pay a net tax of $300 (15 percent of $2,000).

For simplicity's sake, let's assume that each family in our example can take the same $4,000 standard deduction: Jones and Baker are, therefore, allowed to deduct $4,000 from their total incomes, too. It should be obvious that if Jones has four exemptions (worth $8,000) and a $4,000 standard deduction, then he will not have to pay any tax at all on his $12,000 income ($12,000 – $12,000 = $0). Baker's income of $9,000 is the lowest of the three. Baker also has exemptions and deductions of $12,000 and will not have to pay any tax either.

The question of equity now arises. There is a large difference between Jones's and Baker's incomes; why does the government treat them the same? Baker has $3,000 of *unused exemptions and deductions* for which he is getting no financial recognition. If we were to institute the negative income tax, Baker would receive some kind of financial credit for these unused exemptions and deductions; the government would give Baker a **negative tax** (a tax rebate) amounting to some percentage of the $3,000. Friedman has suggested a rebate of 50 percent of any unused exemptions and deductions. Thus, the Baker family would receive a subsidy—a check from the government for $1,500 (50 percent of $3,000). This supplementary income, added to his regular income, would give Baker and his family $10,500 to spend.

Now let's look at Baker's situation if he were to lose his job. What would his subsidy be if he had no income at all? If Baker's exemptions and deductions are worth $12,000, then the family would receive a subsidy of 50 percent of that amount, or $6,000. This figure represents an **income floor.** All families of four in the United States, if they earn no income, would be eligible for this amount. The negative income tax is, in essence, a guaranteed-income plan.

What about incentives? Let's suppose that after Baker lost his job he was offered part-time work at $3,000 a year. Is it to his financial benefit to take the job? From his $3,000 income, he would subtract the same $12,000 in exemptions and deductions ($3,000 − $12,000 = − $9,000) and wind up with a subsidy of $4,500 (50 percent of $9,000 is $4,500). Baker's total income would be this $4500 plus his earned income of $3,000, or $7,500. He *is* financially better off with the job.

Some people might argue that a 50 percent rebate rate (keeping only $0.50 of each earned dollar) is not enough incentive to go to work. But there is nothing in the basic idea that says the percentage must be 50 percent. The percentage could be determined so that families would keep 90 percent (or 100 percent) of the first $5,000 or $6,000 they earned. After this grace period, the percentage might go back to 50 percent. At any rate, the levels of the percentage rates, exemptions, and deduction could be experimentally worked out to provide lower-income families with enough supplementary income to maintain a respectable standard of living and still not destroy work incentives.

We can now begin to see some of the major advantages of a negative income tax. In Friedman's words

> It is directed specifically at the problem of poverty. It gives help in the form most useful to the individual, namely cash. It is general and could be substituted for the host of special measures now in effect.

Let's review its specific advantages. Compared to the present-day welfare system, the negative income tax:

- would cover all in need.
- could be adjusted to guarantee a basic standard of living for every family.
- would help to eliminate the humiliating and dehumanizing aspects of the present system. (Income supplements would be an informal matter, just like receiving a tax refund or a Social Security check; lower-income families would fill out their federal tax forms like everyone else.)

- would be a relatively simple system. (Bureaucratic paperwork, questionnaires, forms, means tests, etc., would be replaced by an uncomplicated income-tax statement.)
- could direct social and rehabilitation workers' efforts toward helping families solve specific problems (jobs, housing, transportation, nutrition, etc.), so that their skills are not wasted on the red tape involved in money transfer.
- would not encourage family breakup.
- would be designed not to discourage people from working.

There are some disadvantages to the negative income tax as well. The program would, in the short run, be more expensive than the present welfare system. More people would be covered, and minimal income levels would probably be higher. Where the money would come from is another matter to consider. When unmarried or divorced women head lower-income households, public opinion strongly supports even greater efforts to collect child-support payments from absentee fathers. **Workfare,** in which able-bodied recipients must accept public-service or private employment, would be a way to keep government subsidy costs down. Friedman does feel, however, that in the long run, the effect of providing a positive work incentive (if the jobs and a continuation of medical assistance are available) and eliminating all other subsidy programs (welfare, food stamps, etc.) would make the cost of a negative income tax lower than the cost of all our existing supplemental income programs combined.

In summary, however we pay for it, we must first decide that we really do want to help the poor. We have the resources, but we seem to lack the public will. A while back, I received an advertisement in the mail called "Shop the Other America." In it was a statement that strongly supported the need for a change in our country's attitude:

> Before we can decide how to accomplish the goal of eliminating poverty, or whether we can afford to do the job, we must first decide that we want to do it—that we will no longer expect children to fill hungry bellies with Kool-Aid and candy, to be the prey of rats, to be weakened with tuberculosis, to grow up amid filth and organized vice, to be taught in deteriorating classrooms by teachers who have lost hope, and that we will no longer allow old people to huddle in lonely, heatless rooms, living on pennies, unable to afford needed medicines and services.

We began this chapter with a strongly worded letter written to a St. Paul newspaper and ended with another statement—equally strong in emotion but light years away in ideology and purpose. Reconciling these two honest, but opposite, views is the unfinished business of us all.

Questions for Thought and Discussion

1. Reread the chapter's opening letter. What is the explanation of why there may be deep resentment directed against the poor? Compare to other sources of public anger such as with the savings and loan scandal or corruption in defense or securities industries. What conclusions can you draw?

2. Is poverty an absolute or a relative concept? Explain.

3. To what degree does the "exploitation of workers" in a capitalist system contribute to poverty?

4. If you were to help decide policies to combat poverty, would you differentiate between those caught in the feminization of poverty versus those poor from structural unemployment? What similarities or differences in policies would you suggest?

5. Check with your local or state welfare department to determine what "means tests" must be met in your city in order to receive welfare assistance.

NEW PERSPECTIVES

Poverty . . . New Perspectives

As we saw in this chapter, the official definition of poverty is basically an income definition, of "falling below the poverty line." But are there, perhaps, other ways to define poverty?

How about "relative poverty" as a working concept? It's interesting to note that during the Great Depression, many American low-income families didn't feel poor because most of their friends and neighbors were essentially in the same boat. On the other hand, is it possible that a middle-income family might feel some degree of relative poverty if they lived among or near ultra-wealthy neighbors? Also, a poverty family in North America (with access to education,

(continued)

food stamps, and probably a television) might easily be considered wealthy by a poor African or Central American family. Consider too a concept that might be called "The Philosopher's Wealth Ratio."

$$\text{Wealth} = \frac{\text{Economic Possessions}}{\text{Economic Desires}}$$

Granted that your wealth ratio might be difficult to calculate scientifically; still, you may have a gut feeling about it. If, for example, your ratio tended to be less than 1, wouldn't you feel poor? On the other hand, if your wealth ratio were greater than 1—no matter what your financial situation—wouldn't you feel relatively contented, even wealthy?"

One writer/philosopher who said that we should try to improve our wealth ratio by reducing the denominator (i.e., desires), was Henry David Thoreau. Throughout his classic, *Walden,* Thoreau keeps coming back to the fundamental economic question: "How can a person do more with less?" More specifically he said, "A man is rich in proportion to the number of things he can afford to leave alone,"* and at one point in his *Journal* he confided,

"My greatest skill is to want but little."

Question: Discuss the factors that might affect your wealth ratio. Consider your income (or potential income), level of skill and education, work ethic, and opportunities for jobs. All of these affect the numerator; i.e., economic possessions. In addition, how does the overall health of the national and international economy fit in? For the denominator (desires), you might evaluate social factors like advertising or where you happen to live. How about the expectations of your family and friends?

Question: If you have the time and inclination, read *Walden.* Does Thoreau's message of "voluntary simplicity" apply to living in the 1990s? Could Thoreau (who was a bachelor) adhere to a simple lifestyle if he had to support children? Discuss.

* Thoreau, Henry. *Walden.* (Reprint. New York: Bramhall House, 1951, p. 97.)

7

Gross Domestic Product

In Chapters 4 and 5, we moved away from the microscopic approach of supply and demand and proceeded to examine the major economic sectors of businesses, households, and government. Now we are ready to take an even broader point of view. This chapter is an introduction to large (macro) economic concepts. It will be as if we were looking at the broad outlines of our economy from some point in outer space, using an "economic telescope" that allows us, in effect, to view the whole picture at once. Economists call this panoramic view of the economy **macroeconomics.**

You probably know quite a bit about macroeconomics already. In fact, you undoubtedly read about it in the newspapers, hear about it on the morning or evening news each day, and listen to arguments about it in every election year. *Macroeconomics* is the study of inflation, unemployment, recession, the gross domestic product (GDP), economic growth, and other broad concepts of an economic system.

Who uses macroeconomic concepts? Our economic soothsayers use them when they attempt to divine the future. Economic forecasters ponder charts and tables like veteran handicappers at the racetrack. They pore over income trends, savings and interest rates, consumer attitudes, change in the money supply, housing starts, automobile sales, birth rates, and other economic and demographic indicators; they then ask such questions as, "Will we have recession or inflation next year—or both?" "Will interest rates go up or down?" "What will happen to productivity?"

Then there are the popular oracles (and sometimes the charlatans) of the various investment markets (stocks and bonds, commodities, and gold and silver) who use macroeconomic concepts to help them predict the ups and downs of their respective markets, where a change of a fraction of a percent can add or subtract thousands of dollars to or from a client's account.

There are also the economic philosophers who ask larger human questions: "Where are we now, and where are we going?" "What is the impact of materialism and technology on the global environment today, ten years from now, or even 100 years from now?" Futurists also utilize macroeconomic ideas and indicators.

Finally, our public officials must know something about macroeconomics. They have immediate, urgent concerns. They are like harried physicians, constantly checking the pulse of the economy, anxious to learn about its strength or weakness, growth or stagnation. These men and women have directly or indirectly accepted the responsibility for maintaining the economic health of the country. They include not only the President of the United States and his staff but also Congress and the decision makers in the hierarchy of the Federal Reserve banking system.

Their economic power is derived from controlling the federal budget, the money supply, and interest rates in response to changing economic conditions. A good understanding of macroeconomics is therefore an excellent tool for intelligent planning and decision making.

Wealth and Gross Domestic Product

Perhaps the best place to start our exploration of this vast area of economic theory and reality is with the idea of **wealth**—a yardstick by which many countries judge each other. Indeed, the United States is the envy of the world because of its tremendous man-made and natural wealth. If we were to add up the value of all our buildings and structures, our equipment and inventories, our land and other natural resources, we would be worth something over 20 trillion dollars (1 trillion is 1000 billion). This figure, however, does not tell us very much about our current economic health. Why? There are two reasons.

First, wealth must be utilized before it can contribute to present-day living standards. Black Africa, for example, has tremendous natural wealth, but this wealth has generally not been utilized and, consequently, most of its people remain economically poor.

Second, the value of a nation's resources in the form of wealth does not necessarily tell us anything about that nation's current production. Without a continuous flow of new goods and services, nations eventually consume their available wealth (like retired couples who use up their savings and are eventually forced to sell their personal belongings to purchase food). Our economy, like a growing family, must have a continuous flow of income and real output if it is to maintain or improve present living standards.

What we are looking for is a concept that goes beyond wealth—a concept that will tell us something about the total output that the nation's land, machines, labor, and management produce year after year. This concept is the **gross domestic product** (GDP). Economists define GDP as: a measure of the final value of all goods and services produced within the nation's borders over a year's time.* Like the amount of our national wealth, GDP is an enormous figure almost too large to comprehend. By the turn of the decade (1990), for example, the total GDP was approximately 5.5 trillion dollars per year!

Perhaps we should pause a moment to consider the difficulties in computing a precise value for the GDP. Of course, much of our total national output can easily be traced simply by adding up total incomes (as shown on our personal income tax returns, for example). There are, however, many goods and services that do not see the light of day and are never officially recorded. An unrecorded cash transaction (designed to bypass the Internal Revenue Service) is one example; billions of dollars in illegal drug trade represent another.

---

* Before 1992, the federal government used the statistic GNP or gross national product. The figure GDP and GNP are not generally different, but GDP is somewhat superior compared to GNP in reflecting the actual production and employment situation within the nation's borders. GDP is also more comparable to what the rest of the world currently uses.

Probably a much larger category of unrecorded production takes place (perfectly legally) under the heading of **nonmarket transactions.** We are all a part of this underground market in one way or another. For example, each time we do something for ourselves that we could have paid someone else to do, our economic activity goes unrecorded in the official GDP statistics. Mary Smith, for example, tunes her old Mustang every six months, but Mary doesn't pay herself (and record it on her income tax form). But if a garage had done the same work, the labor bill might have been $50 or $100. The garage, in turn, would report this amount to the government as service performed, and Mary's tune-up *would* become part of our GDP.

Obviously, these do-it-yourself projects—from growing your own food to remodeling a basement—cannot be accurately accounted for in our national income statistics. The problem posed by nonmarket transactions is considerably amplified when we note the billions of dollars of unpaid household services that are performed mainly by women. Then add to this the billions of dollars of unpaid volunteer services. Although our government does attempt to estimate the value of some of these unrecorded transactions, it is impossible to do this with any precision.

Another problem associated with the GDP is our strong belief in the dictum that "happiness is a rising GDP." We often assume that when GDP is rising, we are all automatically better off. Many economists, however, are now beginning to voice some important concerns about this philosophy.

For example, before we can say we are better off when the GDP goes up, we should look at what is happening to the population during the same period of time. If output rises by 1 percent and population increases by 3 percent, the average family will suffer a *decline* of 2 percent in their standard of living. It's a simple principle that is often ignored, especially in less-developed countries, where population growth frequently outstrips the rise in GDP. One way to overcome this problem is to calculate *per-capita* growth in GDP.

Another point to consider is the distribution of the GDP pie. A rising GDP, for example, may be translated into 25 percent more housing, but if the extra houses are second homes for wealthy families, then we can hardly say that the average citizen is benefiting from this increase in the GDP. Brazil provides us with an exaggerated illustration of this problem. This

South American country has certainly been maintaining a growth economy, but the fruits of its rising GDP have been concentrated mainly in the modern sector. The majority of poor Brazilians, who live in the nonindustrial economy, benefit very little, if at all, from their country's rising GDP. Our generalization that happiness is a rising GDP in this case turns out to be a painful mockery to the poor families who watch their country's income differentials widen as the years go by.

During the 1980s, even Americans discovered that economic growth could disproportionately benefit the wealthiest class of citizens. Government statistics indicate that in 1980, the richest quintile (i.e., the top 20 percent) received 44.9 percent of after-tax income.[24] By 1990, they were receiving 49.7 percent of the total, with the greatest gain going to the top 1 percent; over the decade, this super-wealthy's portion of the "economic pie" went from 8.4 percent to 12.4 percent! Meanwhile the poorest 20 percent of Americans were, in 1990, receiving only 4.3 percent of the total (down from 5.4 percent in 1980).

Of course, a number of families did experience what might be called "quintile hopping," i.e., of moving from a lower economic group to a higher (or from a higher to a lower one). Still, the widening gap of household income distribution in the United States today is generally considered socially and economically unhealthy in a nation that has enjoyed a relatively prosperous and broad-based middle class.

We should also consider the questions of quality. Does the quality of our GDP change over time? Indeed it does. Many people argue that the quality of our merchandise and services has declined over the years; they point to shoddy workmanship, inferior materials, and planned obsolescence as proof of deteriorating product and service quality. Industry might reply, however, that the quality of some products has actually improved. Radios and televisions, for example, are cheaper and more reliable now than they were 20 years ago; radial tires are not only safer but will outlast the tire made 30 years ago; and the computer of today is better, faster, and generally cheaper than the one manufactured a decade ago.

What is your own opinion about the quality of products and services? On balance, has it gone up or down? Either way, product and service quality is an important factor to consider when comparing GDP statistics from year to year.

Instead of looking at individual products, we might also examine the general *composition* of the overall GDP. It has been said, for example, that "if we all came down with cancer, it would boost the GDP." Hospital revenues and the incomes of doctors, nurses, radiologists, and drug companies would go up—at least temporarily. Yet clearly no one could say that we would be better off in such a situation.

Thus, there are economic bads as well as goods. Many economists are beginning to look at GDP growth to try and analyze which expenditures are truly beneficial and which ones are not. For example, it is generally agreed that health-care costs associated with air and water pollution do not add to our net economic well-being, nor do excessive military expenditures.

British economist Leopold Kohr has identified a whole range of products and services that he labels **density commodities.** These goods are purchased by consumers, government agencies, and businesses simply to offset the impact of living in a high-density environment among large-scale social institutions (schools, businesses, cities, etc.).[25] **Density expenditures** include the cost of traffic accidents, many legal services, commuting expenses, escapist media, illegal opiates, prescribed relaxants and stimulants, and the ever more powerful headache remedies ("Life got tougher, so we got stronger," says an Excedrin advertisement). Add to this list the expenditures associated with crime (squad cars, prisons, protective services, exotic burglar alarms and foolproof locks, personalized handguns, mace, etc.), and you begin to get an idea of how much our GDP is devoted to these goods. We are forced to purchase density goods, says Kohr, not because they offer us a net improvement in our standard of living, but because we have evolved into a society in which such goods are necessary to offset the negative side effects of modern urban life. Again, the billions of dollars spent on these types of goods may not add much to the *net* welfare of the population, but they are all counted as part of our official GDP statistics.

Pro-growth versus Anti-growth

Kohr and other maverick economists have actually questioned the prevailing economic ethic that continuous growth is desirable, particularly for the United States and other highly industrialized countries ("the overdeveloped nations," as Kohr calls them). Kohr and those who share his way of thinking are considered advocates of an "anti-growth" or "steady-state" policy that some label "sustainable economics." In this camp, we would also include Herman E. Daly, Paul Ehrlich, and Lester Brown, head of the Worldwatch Institute and author of *Building a Sustainable Society* (W. W. Norton, 1981). All of these economists are concerned with what they see as the results of economic growth: the steady erosion of the quality of the global environment and the decline of the world's nonrenewable resources. Perhaps the extreme point of view comes from Professor Ezra Mishan of The London School of Economics:

> You could very well have stopped growing after the First World War. There was enough technology to make life quite pleasant. Cities weren't overgrown. People weren't too avaricious. You hadn't really ruined the environment as you have now.[26]

Most economists, however, continue to be defenders of growth, agreeing with Adam Smith's historic contention that "the progressive state is in reality the cheerful and the hearty state to all order of society. The stationary is dull; the declining, melancholy."

There is also the view among pro-growth advocates that humans are surprisingly adaptable and that our species has proven over thousands of years that it is capable of making appropriate change when change is warranted. If we run low on certain resources, our market economy (through higher prices) will signal that it's time to find (or create) new substitutes: fiber optics instead of copper, strong (and inexpensive) plastics in place of steel or aluminum; or perhaps a trend toward miniaturization to conserve a myriad of scarce resources. If fossil-fuel supplies become depleted, we will (pro-growth economists say) find substitutes—hydrogen fuel derived from water, for example—or evolve more highly efficient systems with our technological know-how. In this sense, the pro-growth position seems to go hand in hand with what we might call "technological optimism."

We should also pause to consider Irving Kristol's argument that growth is, in fact, a necessary precondition to a racially diverse democracy in which "the expectations of tomorrow's bigger pie, from which everyone will receive a larger slice . . . prevent people from fighting to the bitter end over the division of today's pie."[27] In other words, growth is the economic glue that helps bind the nation while reducing class and ethnic tensions. Defenders of economic growth also point out that very few families can say that they are satisfied with their current economic status. In addition, they remind us that we still have many lower-income people in the United States who are likely to be permanently poor in a zero-growth economy. A final point from pro-growth economists is that it is much easier to deal with pollution in a growing economy; cleaning up the environment will be expensive, and the additional resources must come from somewhere.

Defenders of economic growth are greatly disturbed that an increasing number of people want to go back to the good old days—days that pro-growth people believe were not so good. They ask, "Why can't environmentalists and other anti-growth advocates understand that technology and economic growth are conquering nature for the benefit of mankind?"

Author Mel Ellis, a naturalist who has demonstrated unique sensitivity for both economic and environmental problems, writes

> Man almost literally made the cow, the fat corn kernel, the plump turkey, the beautiful rose. And if he erred in his enthusiasm and polluted his raw materials, his resources, he still made the world enormously better.[28]

Most environmental advocates probably do understand the benefits of technology, progress, and economic growth, but their attention is directed to different concerns; they are listening to different sounds. Essayist E. B. White once summed up this attitude with the comment, "I would feel more optimistic about a bright future for man if he spent less time proving that he can outwit Nature and more time tasting her sweetness and respecting her seniority."[29]

The immediate concerns of environmentalists are not the eradication of poverty or the benefits of high-speed air travel or the advantages of the computer. They do not see a thousand acres of timber as so many completed homes. They see the grandeur of the forest and its enduring value as a generator of oxygen, a climatic stabilizer, and a complex, ecologically diverse habitat for plants and wildlife—and they work for its preservation. Instead of seeing the Appalachian hills as a source of strip-mined coal for heating homes, they ask, "What are the adverse consequences of strip mining for the land and its inhabitants?"

> The D-9 bulldozer is the largest built by the Caterpillar Tractor Corporation. It weighs some 48 tons and is priced at $108,000. With a blade that weighs 5000 pounds, rising five feet and curved like some monstrous scimitar, it shears away not only soil and trees but a thousand other things—grapevines, briars, ferns, toadstools, wild garlic, plantain, dandelions, moss, a colony of pink lady-slippers, fragmented slate, an ancient plow point, a nest of squeaking field mice—and sends them hurtling down the slope, an avalanche of the organic and the inorganic, the living and the dead. The larger trees that stand in the path of the bulldozer—persimmons, walnuts, mulberries, oaks, and butternuts—meet the same fate. Toppled, they are crushed and buried in the tide of rubble.[30]

Along the same line, who could not empathize with novelist James Michener's feelings of sadness and guilt after he returned to the site of his boyhood stream?

> This marvelous stream in which I used to fish and where as a boy I had gone swimming, this ribbon of cool water which has been a delight to generations of farmers, was now a fetid body of yellowish water with not a living thing in it. Frogs, fish, waterlilies, bullrushes, and ducks' nests had all vanished. . . . The loss of my stream had occurred under my nose, as it were, and with me making no protest. When I finally saw what had happened, I was ashamed of my inattention. What in those years had I been doing that was more important than saving a stream? If we continue to abuse and destroy our resources, many of us will be asking that question thirty years from now, but by then it will be too late, and some of the precious things we have lost will not be recoverable.[31]

Environmentalists, in short, are distressed by the ugliness of overdevelopment. They are angered by worldwide pollution in such forms as oil spills and acid rain and also by the growing lists of extinct or endangered species of wildlife. They feel that these are the unnecessary consequences of human selfishness. They are saddened by our blindness—a blindness to the possibility that much of what we value today may be lost forever. Of those who favor development at any cost, they ask, "Why can't you see what uninhibited growth is doing to those things we must preserve for future generations?" The great debate over growth is based on simple but profound differences in values. It will, undoubtedly, remain a public issue of great magnitude for years to come.

GDP and Inflation

We will consider one more major challenge to the attitude that "happiness is a rising GDP." Imagine the following scene: George and Mary Franklin were overjoyed when their joint income increased to $45,000 a year; they had never dreamed they would make that much money. Yet by the end of the year, the Franklin family felt poorer than ever. Not only had they failed to save any money, but Mary Franklin claimed that their standard of living was worse now than it was five years ago. What's wrong?

The answer to this question should be obvious, since we are all adversely affected by the same economic malady. The problem was the rise in the general price level—what economists commonly call **inflation.** Not only does inflation distort and diminish your income, my income, and the Franklins' income, but inflation also distorts the GDP statistics.

A simple example can illustrate this point. Let's assume, for the sake of simplicity, that the U.S. economy produces only one product—wheat. Over a time period of three years, watch what happens to GDP when the price of wheat is inflated from $1 to $5 per bushel:

YEAR	OUTPUT (in bushels)	PRICE (per bushel)	GDP (price × output)
1	3	$1	$3
2	5	4	20
3	9	5	45

Take a look at the GDP column. If someone gave you only the GDP figures $3, $20, and $45, would you say that these figures were a good representation of output? Of course not, because they do not give you the whole story. These GDP figures are, in fact, greatly inflated when you compare them with the increase in actual output of wheat: the GDP has increased to 15 times its original value (from $3 to $45) while output has increased to only three times its original value (from 3 to 9 bushels). In short, if all you saw were these GDP statistics, you would have a very distorted picture of the economic situation. Economists have a name for this distorted or inflated GDP; they call it **money GDP.** Using the same idea, we can now see why Mary and George Franklin felt a little bewildered when they discovered that their money income did not seem to give them any additional purchasing power. Money income and money GDP are, by themselves, inaccurate indicators of the real economic situation.

Unfortunately, money GDP is the figure that is commonly quoted by newspapers, public officials, writers, and teachers. The 1990 total GDP figure of 5.5 trillion dollars mentioned earlier is, in fact, money GDP. Is there any way of getting a more accurate picture of our production? What we need is a more realistic value for the GDP—a GDP figure that does not include inflated prices.

To adjust for inflation in our example, we must compare each year's output with the wheat price of a single base year. We could choose any of the three years for our base, and then apply this base-year price to the outputs of the other two years. For example, let's make year 1 our base. We then multiply the base-year price ($1 per bushel) by the actual output of all three years:

YEAR	OUTPUT (in bushels)	REAL GDP (Year 1 = base year)
1	3	$ 3
2	5	5
3	9	9

The result is **real GDP,** which, as you can see in the table, gives us a far more accurate picture of each year's production than money GDP did.

Of course, the United States does not make one product; it produces millions and millions of goods and services. How can the GDP be adjusted for inflation when there are so many different prices to consider? The same principle applies; economists compare the outputs of all other years to a base-year price. The big difference is that now the price changes of many goods and services (not just one) must be averaged. This average price level can be summarized in a single statistic, called the **price index,** or the **GDP price deflator.** The price index for the base year is always equal to 100, no matter which year we choose. Any change in overall prices is reflected by a change in the price index.

For example, if we use 1987 as the base year (price index = 100) and we find that prices between 1987 and 1990, on average, went up 12.9 percent, then the price index for 1990 would be 112.9. Once we knew that the 1990 index was 112.9, then we would be able to convert 1990 output into 1987 dollars. So suppose you hear someone report that the GDP in 1990 was $5514 billion. You now know that this person is giving you the inflated money GDP figure. How then do you calculate real GDP for 1990? You simply divide the price index for 1990 (112.9) into the money GDP ($5514 billion) and then multiply your answer by 100:

$$\text{Real GDP (1990)} = \frac{5514}{112.9} \times 100 = \$4884 \text{ billion}$$

Now you know the value of real GDP (in 1987 dollars) for 1990. The $4884 billion figure is somewhat less than the inflated $5514 billion figure originally quoted. Unfortunately, the distinction between real and money GDP is rarely made, and the public is often misled by published figures.

We are now prepared for what might be called "The Shortest Economic History Course Ever," as we sum up 60 years of U.S. economic history in less than a page! Look carefully at the chart below. Do you notice any interesting trends in the following figures? (If you read them carefully, you will notice four major economic events in this 60-year history.)

The first significant event is the deflation (a drop in prices) and the Great Depression of the 1930s. In this insecure decade, Americans were faced with high unemployment, a severe drought, and widespread poverty.

The second period of interest is the great upsurge of real economic growth from the early 1940s to the late 1960s. In an accounting sense, this 30-year period was a phenomenal age of American prosperity. In the decade of the 1960s alone, *real* growth per year averaged nearly 4.5 percent! By the middle of this decade, political writer Theodore White would write in his book, *The Making of the President, 1964*:

> There was no doubt that John F. Kennedy and his economists had brought about the first fundamental change in American economic policy since Franklin D. Roosevelt—and the nation glowed

with a boom that was one of the world's wonders. The boom terrified Europeans, angered the underdeveloped in the world, baffled the Russians.[32]

Yet only five years later, after our long Vietnam war, the glow of economic boom and prosperity turned into a bonfire of inflation, the third major event of this 60-year period. During the 1970s, overall prices in the United States rose some 104 percent—a greater increase than in any other comparable period!

And finally, we come to the fourth and most recent period. If the 1970s were characterized by unprecedented inflation, the 1980s was an era of **disinflation,** or a rapid decline in the inflation rate. It began with the initiation of a tight monetary policy in the fall of 1979 and was fortified by two recessions (in 1980 and in 1982), greater international competition in manufacturing, and the collapse of OPEC (the international oil cartel). Few, if any, of America's best economic forecasters predicted the magnitude of this reduction in the inflation rate: from 9 to 10 percent in 1979, 1980, and 1981 down to 3 or 4 percent by the middle of the 1980s.[33] Although it set the stage for a more stable,

YEAR	MONEY GDP (in billions)	GDP PRICE DEFLATOR (1987 = 100)	REAL GDP (in billions)
1930	$90.4	12.0*	$753
1935	72.4	10.5	690
1940	100.1	10.9	918
1945	213.0	13.2	1614
1950	286.7	20.1	1426
1955	403.3	22.9	1761
1960	513.4	26.0	1975
1965	702.7	28.4	2474
1970	1010.7	35.1	2879
1975	1585.9	49.2	3223
1980	2708.0	71.7	3776
1985	4038.7	94.4	4278
1990	5514.0	112.9	4884

1987 = base year

Source: BEA (U.S. Department of Commerce).
*GDP Price Deflator 1930–1955 extrapolated by author.

moderate-growth economy during the rest of the decade, the sudden drop in inflation was initially accompanied by high unemployment and an alarming number of bankruptcies, especially in farm, oil, mining, and related industries.

Thus, unemployment and, at times, inflation mar much of our economic history and continue to plague us as we approach a new century. We will now examine these two extreme economic maladies in more detail in our continuing exploration of macroeconomics.

Questions for Thought and Discussion

1. How difficult would it be to compare the GDP of an industrialized country with the GDP of a Third World country?

2. Carefully think through your own position on the pro-growth versus anti-growth debate. Is there any possibility for compromise? Explain.

3. How would the viewpoints of members of a local chamber of commerce compare with the idea that "happiness is a rising GDP"?

4. What do you think the major economic characteristics or trends of the 1990s will be? Spell out your assumptions.

NEW PERSPECTIVES

Economic Forecasting . . . How Accurate?

Although it's never easy to look into the future, one financial/economic newsletter—Blue Chip Economic Indicators—makes its predictions using an interesting technique: Each month, founder and editor Bob Eggert calls some 50 veteran forecasters from his office in Sedona, Arizona. From the group's individual forecasts, Eggert "forces a consensus" (as he puts it) by averaging the combined projections. The Blue Chip group tackles a variety of key economic items such as inflation, industrial production, housing starts, auto sales, etc. But perhaps their most important statistic is their prediction for the growth of real gross domestic product. Good forecasts are like an early medical diagnosis, that is, information that should help you adapt now to avoid financial illness later. For a businessperson, that lead-time can help prevent expensive mistakes. But how accurate is Blue Chip? How well does this consensus method work?

One way to find out is to calculate the average error over the newsletter's history. Based on forecasts of the preceding October (for the year ahead), the real GDP growth projections have improved from an average error of 1.0 percentage points (after the first 10 years of publication)* down to 0.8 percentage points after 14 years. You may be wondering what a "0.8 percentage point error" means.

To illustrate, assume that Blue Chip's consensus had projected next years growth in real GDP to be 3.0%. Chances are that the actual statistic (released by the Commerce Department a little over a year later) would, on the average, be between 2.2% and 3.8%. Not exactly a bull's-eye, but not too bad either. Especially encouraging is Blue Chip's trend of narrowing its error over time.

Question: If you were asked by Blue Chip to make an individual forecast for next year, how would you do it? What early warning indicators would you devise? For example, to predict a recession, the 3M Corporation uses sales of packing tape as one of their leading indicators. (Can you explain why?) Or how about an increase or decrease in help-wanted ads nationwide?

To predict economic recovery, USAir Group uses sales of airline shuttle tickets. When sales go up, especially in the heavily used business commuter corridors (Boston-New York-Washington, Los Angeles-San Francisco, or Houston-Dallas), it stands to reason that it won't be too long before business activity and production indicators will also be on the rise.**

Other predictive indicators are mentioned in the opening pages of this chapter. For more clues, check the *Wall Street Journal,* or *Business Week* magazine, or perhaps tune in to the commentary on "Wall Street Week."*** From your own methods and criteria, try making a prediction—then check it out a year hence.

---

* Eggert, James. "Consensus Forecasting—A Ten Year Report Card." *Challenge*, July-August, 1987.
**Pearlstein, Steven. "Real-Life Economic Indicator." *St. Paul Pioneer Press*, January 20, 1992.
*** Broadcast every Friday evening over most public television stations.

8

Unemployment and Inflation

What do you think would happen if everyone in the United States woke up one morning and decided to start spending only *half* of the amount of money that they had been spending? This is a very unlikely situation, but let's suppose it really happens. What economic effect would this collective decision produce?

The total impact on the economy would be very large indeed! Let's pull out our economic microscope once again and focus on one small retail store—Joe's Super Sportshop in Plum City, Washington. Joe's business will, in effect, become a microcosm of how businesses will react all across the United States.

First, Joe immediately begins to notice that fewer customers are coming into his store. Before long, he has to let his part-time clerk go. But for Joe himself, so far, so good; he is not yet facing any major problems. As time goes on, however, Joe observes something very disturbing: inventory is piling up. Walking into the storage room, he stumbles over a large box of unsold baseball mitts that he ordered two months ago when business was better. Things are a little more serious now.

Joe decides to try to get rid of his excess mitts by putting them on sale. More importantly (to the economy), he sends a message to the baseball-mitt distributor in Seattle, asking him not to ship any more mitts to the shop.

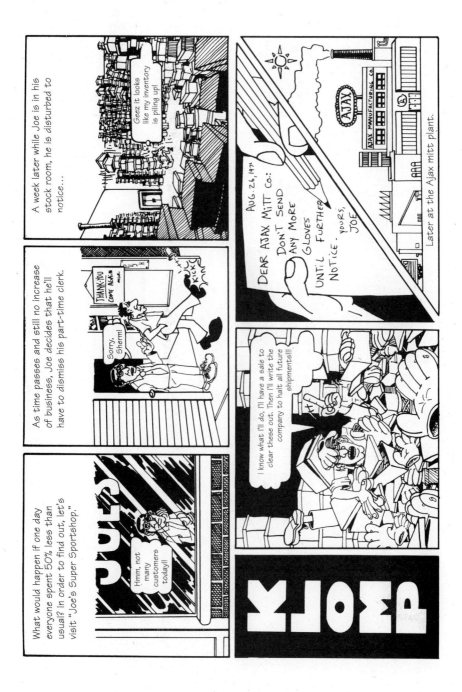

And in an emergency meeting of the board of directors, they even decide.

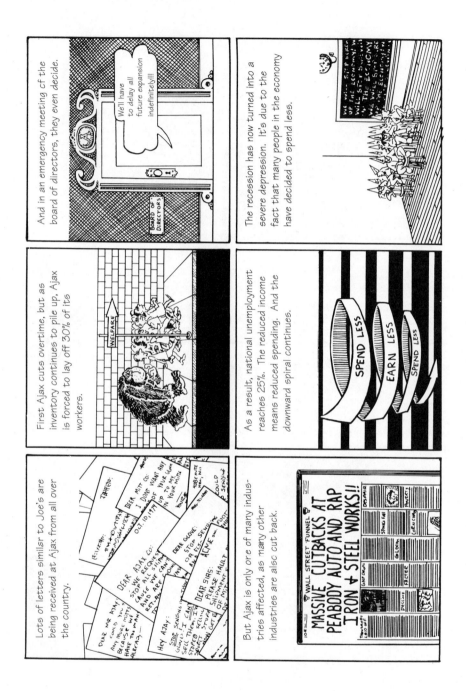

The recession has now turned into a severe depression. It's due to the fact that many people in the economy have decided to spend less.

First Ajax cuts overtime, but as inventory continues to pile up, Ajax is forced to lay off 30% of its workers.

As a result, national unemployment reaches 25%. The reduced income means reduced spending. And the downward spiral continues.

Lots of letters similar to Joe's are being received at Ajax from all over the country.

But Ajax is only one of many industries affected, as many other industries are also cut back.

The bad news is channeled to Ajax Mitt Company in Blackstone, Maine. Ajax, in fact, is getting the same bad news from all of its distributors around the country. At first, Ajax cuts overtime, but its directors soon realize that they must lay off 30 percent of their workers to keep inventory from piling up at Ajax. The directors meet in an emergency session to discuss the new plant that is scheduled for ground-breaking ceremonies next week. They decide to halt all expansion plans indefinitely.

Of course, similar actions are being taken by other industries throughout the nation. Major layoffs are made in the automobile, steel, and housing industries, and orders for new plants and equipment are reduced to a fraction of last year's level. National unemployment soon rises to 25 percent.

With many people on reduced incomes (or no incomes at all), spending falls to lower levels; this downward spiral continues to drag the economy down even further. What is the eventual result of this seemingly simple decision to curtail spending? It has brought on a devastating depression. Thus, recession, depression, high unemployment, and other extreme negative economic swings occur primarily because enough individuals or groups of people somewhere in the economy decide (for any number of reasons) *to spend less*. These people do not necessarily have to be consumers; they can be other major spenders, such as businesses, federal, state, or local governments, or foreign buyers.

Economists summarize the four major categories of spending as:

- consumption expenditures (C)
- investment spending (I)
- government expenditures (G)
- net foreign exports (X_n)

Thus, we can now say that any large reduction in C, I, G, or X_n spending will set forces into motion that can lead to a recession or, possibly, to a depression.

Returning to our example, let's assume we are now going through the economic stage called recession. What is a recession, and how does it differ from a depression?

Recession versus Depression

Economists say we are in a **recession** when the economy experiences at least a *one-half-year period of declining real GDP*. By this definition, our economy has experienced nine recessions since World War II: 1949, 1954, 1958, 1960, 1970, 1974, 1980, 1982, and 1990. In terms of unemployment, our most severe recent recession was in 1982 when, for a number of months, more than 10 percent of the labor force was out of work. The mildest recession was in 1970, with only 5 percent unemployment.

If a recession is a bad cold, a depression is pneumonia. In effect, a **depression** is a severe and prolonged recession. During the Great Depression of the 1930s, which lasted approximately a decade, unemployment rates ranged from 12 to 25 percent (1933).

Depressions have a touch of economic insanity. In the 1930s, idle machines and idle men and women could have been producing goods and services that the nation desperately needed. But the people did no work and the machines rusted—and nobody knew what to do about it.

A comparable tragedy occurred in rural areas. In one part of the nation, fruit and grain ripened and livestock fattened in our great plains and fertile valleys. But some farmers actually destroyed their livestock or burned their grain or let the ripened fruit rot while other people went hungry because they had little or no income and therefore no purchasing power. In her book *The Invisible Scar,* Caroline Bird retells a number of stories that illustrate some of the sadness and suffering during those years:

> Miners tried to plant vegetables, but they were often so hungry that they ate them before they were ripe. On her first trip to the mountains, Eleanor Roosevelt saw a little boy trying to hide his pet rabbit. "He thinks we are not going to eat it," his sister told her, "but we are."
>
> A year after his defeat by Roosevelt, Hoover—who had repeated so many times that no one was starving—went on a fishing trip with cartoonist "Ding" Darling in the Rocky Mountains. One morning, a local man came into their camp, found Hoover awake, and led him to a shack where one child lay dead and seven others were in the last stages of starvation. Hoover took the children to a hospital, made a few phone calls, and raised a fund of $3030 for them.[34]

In addition, disastrous weather conditions in some parts of the country added to the general economic suffering. In the midwestern wheat and corn belt, desperate, bankrupt farmers choked on dust from the worst drought that anyone could remember. Some malicious and sinister force in the air seemed to paralyze all economic activity and turned topsy turvy the economic laws that had always worked for our benefit. This force nearly broke our spirit, a theme John Steinbeck captures so vividly in his classic novel *The Grapes of Wrath* (1939):

> The women studied the men's faces secretly, for the corn could go, as long as something else remained. The children stood nearby, drawing figures in the dust with bare toes, and the children sent exploring senses out to see whether men and women would break. The children peeked at the faces of the men and women, then drew careful lines in the dust with their toes. Horses came to the watering troughs and nuzzled the water to clear the surface dust. After a while the faces of the watching men lost their bemused perplexity and became hard and angry and resistant. . . . Then the women knew that they were safe and that there was no break. They asked, What'll we do? And the men replied, I don't know. . . . But it was all right.

We now know something about that "sinister force." It was initiated by a large reduction in spending in all major sectors of the economy, set off by the great stock market crash of 1929.[35] It then took on a life of its own in an environment of depression psychology interwoven with inept monetary, fiscal, and protectionist trade policies.

This inability of capitalism to avoid the severe effects of the business cycle is, as we noted earlier, capitalism's third tragic flaw. We will soon see how this problem is dealt with in a modern economy. First, however, let's return to our example at the beginning of the chapter.

Remember, we first decided to spend less, then quickly found ourselves in a recession, and later dropped into a deep depression. Now let's assume that after this unhappy time, people, businesses, and government decide to begin spending again. What will it be like at Joe's Super Sportshop?

Joe's business immediately picks up, forcing him to rehire his part-time clerk. He is no longer tripping over surplus boxes of baseball mitts. In fact, when Margie Miller comes in to buy her autographed Lou Gehrig Little League baseball mitt, Joe discovers that he is all sold out. He quickly dials his distributor in Seattle, who quickly writes a purchase order to the Ajax Mitt Company. Ajax receives similar letters from distributors throughout the country. The plant immediately rehires its laid-off workers and gears up for full-capacity production. Finally, the directors of Ajax meet and approve the ground breaking for not one but two new midwestern plants.

Happy times have returned. Things are humming along in all of the economy's major industries. Everyone appears satisfied; more and more expenditures are flowing through the system, buying up greater and greater amounts of goods and services. Notice, too, that once there is upward motion in the economy, everything tends to reinforce this trend. Greater spending generates more employment, more income, and more investment spending. Each of these new spending dollars, in turn, generates another round of spending and enlarged incomes. The pace accelerates—perhaps too fast. At the point that resources become fully employed, the total demand begins to strain the available supply. The result is the beginning of inflation, as more and more dollars chase after a limited supply of output.

At first, of course, there is not much to worry about: A few prices increase here and there as inventories become depleted; product shortages are a little more frequent than before. But when demand begins to expand too fast, the existing plant capacity soon becomes overloaded as our labor force and industrial output become fully utilized. Businesses are under pressure to expand to meet the growing demands for their goods and services, but they simply do not have enough resources to produce all these products. As they attempt to buy existing raw materials and to attract skilled labor, businesses find they have to pay more and more. Labor unions are quick to take advantage of the seller's market for labor, and wages are pushed up. Businesses don't mind too much; they can pass their increased costs on to consumers in the form of higher prices. Inflation that results from higher costs is often referred to as **cost-push inflation.** Higher labor costs, however, mean fatter paychecks. This extra demand pulls prices up again (too many dollars chasing after too few goods), and we experience another round of **demand-pull inflation.**

These two factors (excess demand and higher costs) pull and push the economy again and again, as if bending a wire back and forth. The heated-up economy soon reaches a breaking point. This **hyperinflation** can be as devastating to an economy as a depression; both are extreme economic conditions that can and must be avoided. We will look at these two problems in more detail in a moment, but first let's look at a diagram that shows what we have learned thus far.

Figure 8-1 looks something like the supply and demand graph we examined in Chapter 3. Here, however, the vertical axis represents the overall price level. Any upward movement

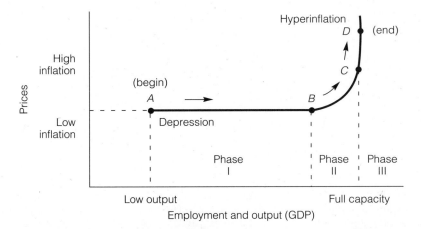

FIGURE 8-1 If we begin at depression point *A* and increase spending, then GDP increases without any inflationary penalty throughout Phase I. If extra spending increases GDP with some inflationary penalty, then we are in Phase II, or the *trade-off area*. Finally, if extra spending results in only higher prices, then we are operating in Phase III.

on the price scale can be directly translated into inflation. The horizontal axis represents output and employment. Both of these values are directly related. If output is high, we know employment will also be high; if output is low, employment will be low.

Let's begin at point *A* (in the midst of the Great Depression). Note the relatively low price level combined with a small GDP and high unemployment. As we begin to spend more, we move along the solid line to the right. Each additional dollar spent increases employment and output without any inflationary penalty. This remains true all the way through Phase I. Once we reach point *B,* any additional spending not only increases output but also creates some degree of inflation. We call this Phase II, or the *trade-off area.* If we want higher levels of output and employment, we must accept a trade-off in the form of higher prices. Once we reach point *C,* however, and continue to spend more and more, we gain nothing in output and employment (because the economy is already operating at full-capacity output), but we completely lose out to hyperinflation.

We might generalize and say that to operate in either Phase I or III is a serious mistake, since we can still gain employment (without any inflation penalty) beyond Phase I, and Phase III represents nothing more than sustained inflation

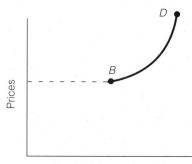

FIGURE 8-2   *Trade-off area* (magnified): Note that prices tend to increase (inflation) when employment increases. On the other hand, if the economy is operating at a low inflationary level, full employment will probably not be maintained.

(with no employment advantage). The logical place to operate (if we are in control of things) is in Phase II, or the trade-off area. Let's magnify this section of our graph (see Figure 8-2) to see precisely how the trade-off area operates.

Trade-Off

In reality, a trade-off is actually a variation of the old saying, "You can't have your cake and eat it too." That is, it's difficult to have full employment and zero inflation at the same time. **Trade-off** forces us to choose the objective that we value most: high employment or low inflation. For example, if we operate at point *B* in the trade-off area in Figure 8-2, we are choosing a low inflation and high unemployment. On the other hand, if we choose an area near point *D*, we are opting for full employment with relatively high inflation.

Sometimes economists prefer to portray this same trade-off problem in a slightly different format, popularly called the **Phillips curve** after A. W. Phillips, who studied historical trade-off data in Great Britain in the 1950s. Instead of plotting employment on the horizontal axis, the Phillips curve plots unemployment, which reverses the curve but shows essentially the same trade-off concept. In Figure 8-3, a Phillips curve indicates unemployment and inflation from 1964 to 1969. Take a careful look at the general shape of the Phillips curve, and note how it portrays the trade-off concept.

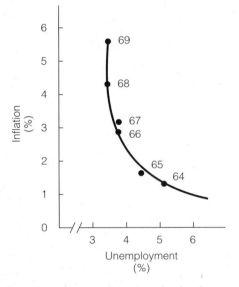

FIGURE 8-3 The *Phillip's curve* indicates a fairly clear trade-off between the inflation rate and the unemployment rate in the United States for the years 1964–1969.

Over some time periods, as in Figure 8-3, a Phillips curve will show a fairly good trade-off relationship; over other time periods, the relationship will not be so neat and tidy. Still, government policymakers must often contend with the trade-off dilemma and make some tough choices. The comment "If we are ever going to solve our terrible inflation problem, we may have to have a recession" is an example of the sort of painful choice that sometimes must be made when dealing with a severe economic problem. How is such a choice made? For example, which problem—inflation or unemployment—is going to give the economy more trouble? Economists can't say for sure because each problem affects us differently. So, let's take a closer look at the specific economic impacts of both of these economic maladies.

Inflation

Exactly why is inflation bad? Most people have jobs during high inflationary periods, and inflation alone normally does not reduce output. The problem is that **inflation** distorts the economy; it redistributes large portions of the economic pie away from some people and places that income into the hands of others—often unfairly or free of charge.

Indeed, some groups fare well during inflationary times. Anyone on a flexible income, for example, will usually do all right. Workers represented by labor unions with bargaining clout (and inflation-based escalator clauses in their contracts) tend to benefit. Large corporations may also profit. Since demand is usually high, during an inflationary period, businesses are often able to raise their prices in response to higher labor and raw-materials costs. Speculators who purchase property, gold, rare coins, paintings, or other inflation hedges at bargain prices and then sit back to let inflation do its work also reap financial rewards from inflation. Finally, borrowers of large amounts of money often find themselves in good shape during an inflationary period because they can pay back their loans in inflated dollars, which are relatively easy to come by.

It shouldn't be difficult to see which groups are the hardest hit by inflation. Fixed-income families suffer the most. These include, among others, the millions of marginal workers in low-paying, nonunion industries, retail clerks, hotel and restaurant workers, and others who work at or below the minimum wage.

Since borrowers gain as a result of inflation, lenders often lose out; so do savers, who watch (with great frustration and bitterness) their saved-up purchasing power evaporate under the heat of rising prices. The so-called virtues of a nation—hard work and thriftiness—become cruel hoaxes, and the vices of speculation and excessive borrowing are rewarded. Inflation becomes a silent economic disease that saps incentives—a disease that renders people unsure of the present economic reality and fearful of what the economic future will bring.

Unemployment

Now let's look at the other side of the trade-off dilemma—**unemployment.** To be unemployed means more than just not having a job. By definition, a person is unemployed if he or she is *actively seeking employment but cannot find work.* To find out who is unemployed, the U.S. Census Bureau samples numerous households each month, asking the key question, "Have you been actively looking for work in the past four weeks?" If the person answers yes but has not been able to secure either part-

or full-time employment, then he or she is considered officially unemployed by the federal government.

Surprisingly, not all unemployment is undesirable or harmful to the economy. Economists say that **frictional unemployment** affects about 4 percent of the labor force; people in this category are looking for work for the first time or are voluntarily changing jobs. They are actively seeking work, but their situation is not terribly serious. In fact, without some frictional unemployment, our economy would lose the measure of efficiency that is brought about by **labor mobility.** Since there is no way to reduce this kind of unemployment (and we would not necessarily want to), we can say that our economy is fully employed when we are at or near this 4 percent level. Putting it slightly differently, when 96 percent of all potential working people are employed, we can say that the labor force is operating at or near full capacity.

However, other categories or types of unemployment are more serious and often more intractable. For example, at any given time, there is a group of unemployed people that economists call **discouraged workers** who have simply given up hope of finding work. Although we don't know who all of these discouraged workers are, they include married, college-educated women who would like a good job but can find nothing available where they live and lack the mobility to move to where the jobs are. And there are middle-aged men and women who are fired, phased out, or indefinitely laid off; these individuals may have worked for years but now find that no one wants to hire them. There are also many Americans from minority groups who have simply given up trying to find jobs because of racial discrimination. These are just a few examples of the disappointed dropout workers who exist in an economic limbo.

Then there are the **structurally unemployed.** We already learned something about this group in Chapter 6. They are workers whose skills became obsolete or whose jobs disappeared when local businesses shut down or moved away. The problems of the structurally unemployed cannot be readily solved by more spending and greater economic expansion. These workers need to be retrained in new skills and often need assistance to relocate to areas where jobs are available.

Finally, we come to **Keynesian unemployment,** named after British economist John Maynard Keynes (1883–1946). This kind of unemployment results from a *lack of spending* and the resulting downturn of the business cycle (described at the beginning of the chapter). Keynes first devised the theory that this type of unemployment can be significantly reduced by *instituting government programs designed to stimulate additional spending.* This was indeed a revolutionary idea, as few economists before Keynes had ever dreamed of manipulating an economic system.

Of course, Western economies had always experienced the business cycle (wide swings from unemployment to inflation and back to unemployment), but nineteenth- and early twentieth-century economists (often called **classical economists**) felt that an economy would automatically correct itself. It had to (they thought), because when output is produced by businesses, an equivalent amount of income must be generated by that production. As French economist Jean Baptiste Say (1767–1832) states in his famous **Say's Law,** "Supply creates its own demand."

So what did classical economists say would happen if we suddenly experienced a significant downturn in the business cycle, resulting in high unemployment? They reasoned that the unsold output would eventually force prices down. Low prices would, in turn, stimulate demand, and businesses would soon be rehiring their laid-off workers.

But what would happen if some people didn't get their jobs back? The classical economists had a logical answer for this, too. The lower wage would create an incentive for cost-conscious businesspeople to hire workers. The wage rate might drop considerably, but eventually everyone would be back at work, or so the reasoning went. The classical economist thought the worst thing that could happen to this neat, self-correcting system was to allow government to interfere. In short, the bywords of the classical age might have been "Stay cool and everything will take care of itself."

But then the Great Depression arrived. Something was terribly wrong. Unemployment went from bad to worse—and stayed that way year after year. Prices dropped; so did wages and interest rates. But there were no consumer spending sprees, and businesses did not invest or rehire the unemployed, even at the lower wage rates. Farmers found prices so low that at times they didn't bother to haul their crops to market. Incomes were so depressed that few consumers had sufficient purchasing power to buy up what was available. The nation was running out of patience. You don't stay cool for five years or more when you are out of work. What we needed was a new theory that worked. The time was ripe for the genius of John Maynard Keynes. Let's examine his theory in greater detail.

Keynes and the Great Depression

To understand Keynes's ideas fully, we must develop a new model of the economy. It will be something like our single market model from Chapter 3, except that now we must consider the markets for all goods and services. When we talk about "total supply," we mean real GDP. When we speak of "total demand," we mean the sum of all types of spending: consumption, business investment, government, and net foreign spending.

What would the **total supply curve** look like in our new model? Recall that the single market supply curve (such as Figure 3-5 in Chapter 3) describes how much of one product suppliers want to provide at different prices. We now want that same information with respect to total supply, but this time we are dealing with the variables of **spending** and **output,** not price and quantity.

Thus, we ask the suppliers (all businesses), "If total spending were $4 trillion, how much output (GDP) would you want to supply?" It should be obvious that if total spending ($C + I + G + X_n$) were at a level of $4 trillion, businesses would theoretically want to supply the same amount ($4 trillion) of GDP (see Figure 8-4a). Stated another way, suppliers would only produce $4 trillion of GDP if they thought consumers would buy it up.

All the other points on our total supply curve (see Figure 8-4b) are quite easy to locate. For example, if there were $8 trillion worth of spending ($C + I + G + X_n$), then businesses would want to supply $8 trillion worth of GDP output. In general, businesses would want to match any amount of spending with an equivalent amount of GDP supply. Each point dot on the total supply curve therefore falls on a straight line equally distant from both the output and spending axes. Our total supply curve (which doesn't really curve) therefore begins in the lower left corner and shoots straight up to the right at an angle of 45°.

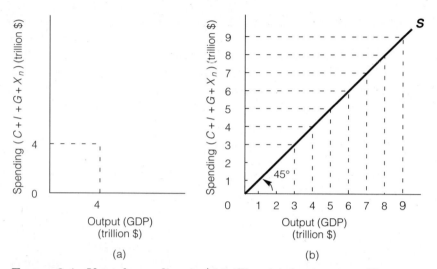

FIGURE 8-4 If total spending is $4 trillion (a), businesses will want to supply $4 trillion in GDP. At other levels of spending (b), businesses will also want to match each dollar amount spent with an equivalent amount of GDP output. The resulting aggregate (total) supply curve rises at a 45° angle.

Now let's look at total demand. To construct our **total demand curve,** we must ask ourselves, "How do spenders react to changes in their incomes?" Let's look at an example. Suppose your individual income last year was $9,000, but your income this year was reduced to $4,000. What would happen to your spending pattern for this year? Most people faced with this situation would probably spend more than the $4,000 income (in the short run at least). Let's say that you spend $8,000, even though your income is only $4,000. (For a while, therefore, you will be dis-saving—borrowing money.) This point, which lies in the lower left corner of the individual demand curve in Figure 8-5, represents something over $8,000 in spending but only $4,000 in income. Now suppose that you move up the income scale; your income is now $16,000, and you find that you are spending all of it. We will label this point on our demand curve "no savings." Finally, at a $32,000 income, you are able to save some money because you are spending only $24,000.

But what about the overall economy? Will the shape of the total demand curve, which comprises $C + I + G + X_n$, be similar to the demand curve in Figure 8-5? Yes. It is reasonable to assume that when our incomes are suddenly reduced, we tend to spend more (at least in the short run); if our incomes suddenly go

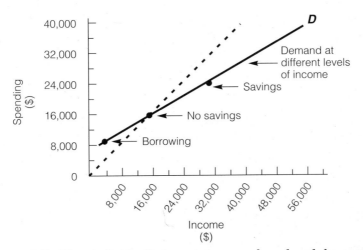

FIGURE 8-5 If an individual's income is severely reduced, he or she will tend to borrow money in the short run (note the point in the lower left corner of the individual demand curve). A short-term rise in individual income makes savings more likely. At the no savings point somewhere in between these two income levels, a person's income is exactly equal to his or her spending.

up, we are more likely to save. Community spending patterns are therefore similar to the spending patterns of individual families.

Now let's see what the total supply curve and the total demand curve look like together. In Figure 8-6, note that we have added GDP (total output) to total income on the horizontal axis. You may wonder how we can equate both concepts. Are they the same?

Yes; for every dollar's worth of output, a dollar's worth of income is generated. Thus, if we added up the incomes from all economic activity (wages, rents, profits, and interest), the total would be equivalent to the final value of our goods and services (GDP). Take, for example, the chair you are presently sitting in. Isn't its final price a "summary" of all the different incomes that went into producing and distributing the chair? We therefore say that total income equals GDP.

Returning to Figure 8-6, we can see that there is an equilibrium level of income (point *B*) at which aggregate (total) supply crosses aggregate demand (just as in Chapter 3 we had an equilibrium for the supply of, and demand for sweet corn). To prove that point *B* must be the equilibrium level, let's see what happens when we are not at this point.

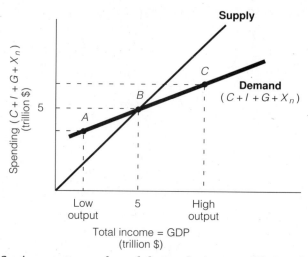

FIGURE 8-6 *Aggregate supply and demand:* at an equilibrium level (point *B*), the dollar value of GDP supplied ($5 trillion) is equal to the dollar value of total spending. If the economy temporarily functions at point *A* or point *C*, then market forces tend to move the economy back to equilibrium point *B*.

At point *A*, we find that the spending level $(C + I + G + X_n)$ is greater than the amount of output produced. No equilibrium level of income can be achieved under these conditions, because if spending is greater than output, businesses must crank up production to meet the surplus demand. (Remember that businesses want to supply whatever is demanded.) Thus, at point *A*, forces are set in motion that push output to higher levels (that is, toward point *B*).

The economy can't remain at point *C* for very long either. Here, the spending level is less than the amount of output. This situation forces producers to cut back on output, reducing GDP, and we soon return to the equilibrium level of income. *B* is the only point on our graph at which output exactly matches the level of spending; it is therefore the only point we might characterize as a **stable equilibrium.**

We are now ready to appreciate and understand Keynes's great discovery. Keynes saw that an economic system might be in a stable equilibrium at a *depression level of GDP.* Graphically, this means that if the supply curve crosses through the demand curve at a low level of national income, the economy could settle in for years and years. Classical economists talked endlessly about declining wages and prices in the 1930s, but these same self-regulating mechanisms never pulled the economy out of the worst depression in U.S. history. What we needed was a new theory and, even more important, new activist policies to deal with the punishing economic realities.

Fiscal Policy

What was Keynes's prescription? If we closely study the total supply-demand graph, we should be able to see what Keynes had in mind. What is needed is to "lift up" the total demand curve to the point at which supply crosses demand at a *full-employment level of GDP*. Let's see how this would look on our supply-demand graph (see Figure 8-7).

Keynes's basic prescription for lifting the total demand curve was to have the government stimulate demand by injecting new spending into the economy in one of two ways:

1. by increasing government spending G (without altering taxes)
2. by decreasing taxes (without altering government spending, thereby increasing consumption expenditures C)

Either or both of these **fiscal** (budgetary) **policies** will shift the total demand curve upward, as we can see in Figure 8-7.

Now look closely again at this figure. Do you notice anything unusual? A careful examination of the upward shift in demand shows that a relatively *small* increase in spending results in a *large* increase in income and output. For example, a $10 billion increase in government spending might result in a $20 billion (or greater) increase in GDP. In short, any extra dollars spent are supercharged dollars! Economists call this the **multiplier effect.**

Why are these new spending dollars multiplied? Let's consider an example. If the government cuts my taxes by $5, my personal income will increase by $5. I may spend all or part of that $5. Let's say I save $1 and spend the rest. My $4 expenditure suddenly becomes extra income for someone else (perhaps the plumber who fixed my leaky kitchen sink). The plumber, in turn, may save a little of this extra income and spend the remainder,

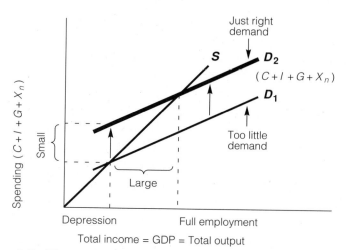

FIGURE 8-7 *The Keynesian solution:* if there is insufficient total demand in the economy (D_1), a depression may be avoided if the government institutes policies to increase total spending to D_2. Note that a relatively small increase in demand can create a relatively large increase in GDP. This is called the *multiplier effect.*

as will the next person, and the next. Now if $4 of extra spending has a supercharged effect, so will an extra $5 billion, or $50 billion. Of course, this effect can work in reverse, too; a $5 billion reduction in spending will obviously reduce GDP by much more than the original $5 billion.

Although the strategy to cure a recession can be rather simply stated—increase government spending and reduce taxes—the administration of these policies is another story. Any time you adjust expenditures and taxes you are tampering with the federal budget. What would the impact on our federal budget be if we lowered taxes and simultaneously increased government expenditures? We would obviously have a **deficit,** and budgetary deficits are usually considered bad economics. Indeed, in the 1930s, "spending your way into prosperity" seemed rather odd to some and even dangerous to others. The federal budget, according to the prevailing thought, simply had to be balanced.

The Great Depression of the 1930s might therefore have been avoided by federal budgetary manipulation. Even as recently as the Kennedy administration, members of Congress were not totally receptive to the idea of stimulating the economy

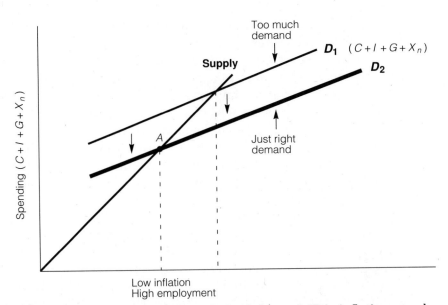

Figure 8-8 If there is too much total demand (D_1), inflation may be avoided if the government sets up policies to reduce total demand to a noninflationary level of GDP (D_2).

with a tax cut. However, when the Kennedy tax bill was passed in 1964, the sluggish economy steamed ahead with such speed that the taxes collected on higher incomes eventually paid back the deficit incurred by the original tax cut.

It was, in fact, the spending for the Vietnam War *and* expensive social programs (in the late 1960s) plus the huge upsurge in OPEC oil prices (during the mid-1970s) that spoiled what might have been an age of real economic growth with only moderate inflation. Instead, the decade of the 1970s brought Americans a new and painful period of high inflation.

What would Keynes have said about inflation? What fiscal policies would be in order now? To answer this, let's take a look at how the problem of inflation affects the graph of total supply and total demand (see Figure 8-8).

Obviously, the problem is now *too much demand*. The economy is producing at full capacity (maximum output), but the spending level is even greater than the available GDP. It's a classic example of demand-pull inflation, when "too many dollars are chasing after too few goods."

Looking at Figure 8-8, we see that demand curve D_1 intersects the supply curve S far above the point of full-employment GDP and should be brought down to a noninflationary point. Although we may not be able to achieve the ideal of zero inflation and full employment at the same time (recall the trade-off problem), there is no reason why we cannot aim for minimal inflation with relatively high employment (point A).

The correct anti-inflationary prescription to pull demand down is to raise taxes, lower government spending, and generally work toward a budgetary **surplus.** Indeed, this solution seems relatively simple. So why is it so difficult to administer an anti-inflationary economic policy?

To come to grips with the problem of inflation, we must understand the realities of the political process, since fiscal policy is ultimately decided by the President and the Congress. Let's return for a moment to Keynes's prescription for combating unemployment. Although there were some qualms about budgetary deficits at one time, the remedies themselves (cutting taxes and increasing spending) can be almost enjoyable for a politician. Everyone likes a hefty tax cut, and special-interest groups—from the Army to the Peace Corps, from the poverty worker to the peanut farmer—thrive on additional spending programs. So the cure for a recession is kind of a welcome problem, because every politician from the President on down stands to gain in popularity with each new tax cut, each new subsidized program, and each additional worker put back on the job.

Inflation is something else, however. Following up on the economists' recommendations to increase taxes and cut programs and entitlements like Social Security can be political suicide. In fact, a number of economists have concluded that the Keynesian remedies for inflation are simply inoperable because of these political realities.

Thus, until the 1970s, we could say that the Keynesian revolution in economic policy gave us a good measure of economic security. Indeed, the United States has been pretty good at avoiding serious economic downturns since the 1930s. Most economists felt then that unless new and unknown factors (war, global drought, a world debt crisis, etc.), occurred in the near future, the United States would probably never live through another Great Depression—thanks, in a large part, to Keynes.

But then the 1970s arrived, with an energy crunch and unacceptable rates of inflation. Suddenly Keynesian policies did not seem to be working. Not only was there political paralysis in dealing with inflation (including the failure of price-wage controls), but the country was also moving toward a new era of inflation *and* recession combined. By the mid-1970s, we were hearing the ominous word **stagflation** (stagnation + inflation) more and more. By 1975, it was apparent that for the first time in our history, we would have inflation rates of greater than 8 percent, combined with a bonafide recession. Some economists were advocating contractive fiscal policies to combat inflation; others wanted just the opposite—large tax cuts to help put people back to work. In short, there were no longer any simple Keynesian remedies.

Supply-Side Economics

Thus, the stage was set in the early 1980s for a new approach—**supply-side economics**—to emerge. Supply-side theory revolves around two key ideas that are intimately intertwined: economic incentives and economic growth. More specifically, it assumes that what our stagflated economy needs is not an additional spending stimulus but greater incentives to improve the supply of goods and services.

The government (under the Reagan administration) chose to encourage these incentives by reducing overall tax rates. The centerpiece supply-side legislation, initiated in 1981 and reinforced in 1986, included large, across-the-board, individual tax-rate cuts designed to stimulate work efforts and generate greater savings. It was hoped that these reforms would (in the long run) translate into more investment spending and that this additional investment plus the work incentive would, in turn, enhance the nation's productivity (output per worker). Improved productivity might then moderate inflation and promote growth. Finally, the resulting growth (according to supply-side theory) would generate such a large increase in the nation's income that the additional tax revenues would eventually pay back the short-term loss of revenue caused by the lower tax rates. If everything worked as intended, a balanced budget and higher growth and productivity would be achieved without any inflationary penalty.

Supply-side recommendations also included offering greater incentives for business investment and for research and development and reducing the web of government regulation that often frustrates business activity and adds to production costs. Supply-side theorists claimed that far too much attention was being paid to stimulating the demand side of the economy, to enforcing cumbersome regulations, and to evolving a tax system that discouraged saving, risk-taking, and work effort, thereby diminishing the supply side of the equation.

Actually, supply-side economics is not an entirely new idea. French economist Jean Say emphasized supply, which he was certain would "create its own demand" sooner or later. Economic philosophers David Hume (1711–1776) and Charles Montesquieu (1689–1775) warned their eighteenth-century readers that excessive tax rates would result in a diminishing work effort. In fact, perhaps no one described the central thesis of supply-side economics better than Montesquieu, when he wrote:

> Nature is just to all mankind; she repays them for their labors; she renders them industrious because she attaches the greatest recompense to the greatest works. But if an arbitrary power snatches away the rewards of nature, one will learn distaste for work, and inactivity will appear to be the only good.[36]

Montesquieu's sentiments undoubtedly hit a responsive chord among Reagan's economic theorists, who were eagerly looking forward to the predicted benefits of the supply-side tax legislation and other initiatives.

Unfortunately, however, these supply-side policies did not achieve many hoped-for goals. For one thing, annual federal deficits had ballooned to unheard of heights by the end of the Reagan era. The **public debt** (the summation of all yearly federal deficits) nearly tripled from $909 billion in 1980 to $2.6 trillion in 1988. Nor did the U.S. savings rate improve. In fact, for a number of years, it actually declined. And productivity—a key to long-run inflation control and ultimately to our overall standard of living—continued at a low and worrisome rate. From 1980 to 1988, productivity increases averaged only 1.3 percent per year (about the same rate as in the 1970s and only one half the rate of the 1960s). These were all, most experts agree, serious and continuing problems.

On the positive side of the performance ledger, the Reagan

administration (with decisive help from the Federal Reserve System) had reduced the inflation rate significantly by 1983; thereafter, Americans enjoyed not dramatic growth, but steady improvements in the real GDP for 92 straight months (November 1982 to July 1990), plus relatively low joblessness. Economists disagree as to whether supply-side policies should be credited for this economic growth or whether the credit should go to old-fashioned Keynesian deficit spending, combined with a concurrent expansion of consumer and business debt. Indeed, such interpretations are part of a continuing and healthy debate among economists and others who are concerned about the direction and performance of our economy.

Recall, too, that another group of economists see the future as a period of dwindling global resources and are skeptical about the possibility of continued economic expansion. Their ideas, in contrast to those of Reagan supply-siders and Keynesian demand-siders, revolve around how to rearrange the economic system so that we can be reasonably well off without continual exponential economic growth.

At any rate, new theories eventually supersede the old. Creative and innovative ideas, combined with specific policies to deal with changing economic conditions, are continually needed. Hence, we will always be looking for economic philosophers like Adam Smith or John Maynard Keynes—this time, however, for one who can match wits with our own troubled times.

Questions for Thought and Discussion

1. What are some solutions for "stagflation"?

2. As the Cold War winds down, economists talk about a "peace dividend." If the nation had a peace dividend of $100 billion dollars, how, in your opinion, should we use it? List priorities and defend your list.

3. How can we say that output equals employment when they are not expressed in the same units of measure?

4. In the 1960s it was not uncommon to hear the opinion: "We need a war to maintain our prosperity." Evaluate this statement in terms of your knowledge of fiscal policy and recent economic history.

NEW PERSPECTIVES

How Much . . . The Public Debt?

Throughout history, individuals, families, and nations, too, have been warned about taking on too much debt. Consider the Old Testament's "The rich ruleth over the poor, and the borrower is the servant to the lender." (Proverbs 22:7) Of more recent concern, Harvard economist Benjamin Friedman, in a 1988 critique of Reaganomics, wrote the following:

> The trouble with an economic policy that artificially boosts consumption at the expense of investment, dissipates assets, and runs up debt, is simply that each of these outcomes violates the essential trust that has always linked each generation to those that follow. We have enjoyed what appears to be a higher and more stable standard of living by selling our children's economic birthright.*

Nonetheless, total U.S. government borrowing continues to rise. The focal point for concern has been Washington's accumulated chronic deficits—or what is commonly called "the public debt." At the turn of the decade (1990), the dollar value of our public debt was an astonishing $3.2 trillion and still climbing. (Remember that a trillion is a thousand billion!)

One way to get a feeling for all that borrowed money is to take a moment and reflect on a visual image: More specifically, what would the public debt look like if it were stacked in a single pile in your back yard?**

Question: Calculate how high you would have to pile $1,000 bills to create a stack worth $3.2 trillion. (Hint: a million dollars of tightly packed $1,000 bills would be roughly four inches high, and also don't forget that a mile is 5280 feet.)

Perhaps a more scientific way of looking at the national debt problem is in relative terms, that is, of measuring it in relation to economic productive capability. (For example, a $20,000 debt for a millionaire is a trifle, but the same amount for a low-income person might be a financial catastrophe.)

Question: In relation to U.S. productive capacity, calculate the 1990 public debt ($3.2 trillion) as a percent of money GDP for 1990 ($5.5 trillion). What about a decade earlier? The public debt in 1980

---

* Freidman, Benjamin M. *Day of Reckoning: The Consequences of American Economic Policy Under Reagan and After,* p. 4. New York: Random House, 1988.

** Idea from Larry Burkett's *The Coming Economic Earthquake,* p. 57. Chicago: Moody Press, 1991.

was $.91 trillion with a money GDP of $2.7 trillion. Calculate the debt as a percent of 1980's GDP and compare it with the 1990 figure. (You may also wish to update your figures for the most recent year.) Discuss a plausible scenario that would solve or help solve the debt problem in the long run. Include in your answer an assessment of the political problems including the tax/expenditure trade-offs and sacrifices that the nation might have to endure if your plan were taken seriously.

9

Money

Imagine that you and 50 friends, acquaintances, and relatives are all shipwrecked on a large, lovely island in the middle of the South Pacific. At first, it is an idyllic life as everyone lounges on the sunny beach waiting for the rescue ship to sail into view, but after a few days you begin to realize the seriousness of your predicament. With grim faces, everyone gathers on the beach to map out some kind of survival plan.

A governing body is elected, and soon the necessary tasks are taken up by different individuals. Since Joe Jones is a carpenter, he volunteers to build thatched huts for everyone. Smith and Baker are assigned to make fishing boats and nets. Chester Olson will gather wild foods for the community larder.

Time passes. The island economy becomes more specialized and complex. Before too long, however, major problems arise as people experience bottlenecks in their transactions. Some individuals become frustrated when they attempt to get their thatched roofs mended or to obtain food for the evening meal. What's wrong?

The problem is that our little economy has become more and more complex, to the degree that now some kind of monetary system is needed. Early on, the islanders used the **barter system,** freely exchanging goods and services when needed.

1st day

Dear Journal:
There are 50 of us now stranded on this island due to our shipwreck. Weather's sunny and rescue boat is due soon. Found a polaroid camera.

2nd day

We elected a governing body today and assigned tasks to everyone. Joe will be building huts, Smith & Baker will be making fishing boats & nets, and Chester will be hunting for wild foods.

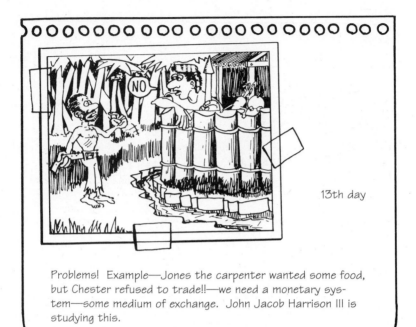

13th day

Problems! Example—Jones the carpenter wanted some food, but Chester refused to trade!!—we need a monetary system—some medium of exchange. John Jacob Harrison III is studying this.

15th day

John Jacob Harrison III's report: Money must be durable, easily transferred, divisible, have limited supply, and be easily duplicated only by the island bank.

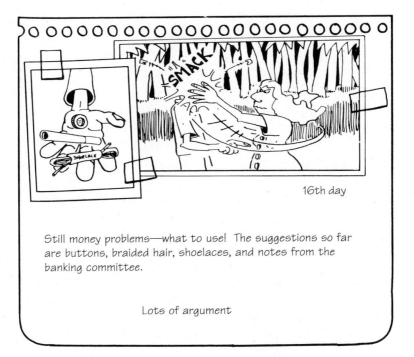

16th day

Still money problems—what to use! The suggestions so far are buttons, braided hair, shoelaces, and notes from the banking committee.

Lots of argument

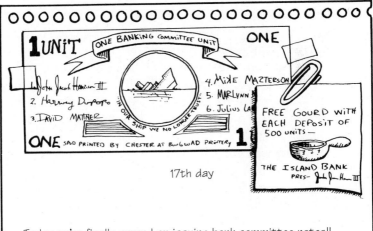

17th day

Today we've finally agreed on issuing bank committee notes!! They will be our official monetary units—each one will contain the signatures of each member of our banking committee.

This works fine on a limited scale, but when a few more jobs are assigned to a few more people, the community begins to encounter some major problems.

As an example, suppose that your specific skill is mending clothing. One day you decide you would like some of Chester's wild foods, and you propose to trade your services for part of Chester's specialty. Unfortunately, Chester tells you he doesn't need any of his clothing mended; what do you do? In a moneyless economy, you must find a third party who not only needs clothing mended but also has a service that Chester wants. If you can't find that third person, you may be out of luck. Trying to track down all the people that you need to make all the exchanges you require would be time-consuming and exhausting. And, in the long run, you still might not locate the necessary people to make your final exchange.

Thus everyone on the island is becoming more and more convinced of the need to develop some kind of monetary system; why? Simply because it will make it considerably easier to exchange goods and services. When **money** is effectively doing its job, it functions as a universally accepted medium of exchange. It also acts as a standard of value. As such, a **money supply** has a single monetary unit (for example, a dollar) that is a common denominator for all economic goods and services. (It's really amazing, for example, that we can use the same unit of currency to compare a dollar's worth of hamburger with a billion-dollar space telescope.) Finally, money can be used as a store of value. It can be saved or spent, hoarded or invested. It's a marvelous tool, and, without a doubt, one of civilization's most useful inventions.

The islanders elect a banker (John Jacob Harrison III) and give him the responsibility of devising a monetary system for the island. Since John has never thought much about the characteristics of money, he forms a banking committee to discuss the issue. "First, let's list the different attributes that our new money system should have," John says, as the committee sits down for a meeting. Baker makes the first point: "Whatever we use for money must be fairly *durable* and something that can be *easily transferred* from person to person." Everyone nods in agreement.

After a moment's silence, Joe Jones suddenly says, "There must be a basic unit (like the dollar) that can be *divided into smaller units* as well as *multiplied* into larger units, right?" The group feels that although this is a sound point in theory, it is impractical on the island, where supplies of suitable materials for money are limited.

Chester, sitting off by himself, is thinking very hard about something. He suddenly stands up and says, "Hold on, hold on. The most important thing about money is its *limited supply*— too much of the stuff will make it worthless." Everyone is impressed by Chester's insight. John (the banker) says, "You're absolutely right, Chester, but you haven't gone far enough." There is a hushed silence as John formulates his thoughts and then continues: "Yes, our money supply must be limited, but we must also be able to expand the amount of money in the economy as the economy itself expands. We have a problem here," the island banker continues, "because whatever we use for money must be easy for us (the authorized bankers) to duplicate but very difficult or impossible for any unauthorized person to counterfeit. Therefore, we need to be very careful in our choice of what to use as money."

Baker thinks that we could use buttons as monetary units. "The banking committee would need authorization to remove all the buttons from the islanders' clothing. . . ."—but before Baker can say another word, he is told to sit down and think of something else. Someone else suggests shoelaces, pointing out that the laces could be cut up into different denominations. Other suggestions include everything from braided hair to pieces of paper signed by the banking committee. It might be worth our while to pause here, leave the island for a moment, and delve a little deeper into the actual history of money. You may wonder where in fact did it get its first foothold? And how did it evolve into the monetary systems of today? Let's take a closer look.

The Origins of Money

No one knows for sure, but it's quite likely that the earliest medium of exchange was what economists call **commodity money**—money that has intrinsic worth in the form of some kind of valuable commodity. Some archaeologists suggest that the first commodity money may have been a certain standardized quantity of grain that was grown in small farming communities approximately 10,000 years ago. Such a scenario implies that some sort of standardized measure of grain became the commonly accepted standard of value. We do know that roughly 4000 years ago, the Babylonian Code of Hammurabi specified that unskilled workers were to be paid in grain, and archaeological research has revealed that grain banking was prevalent in ancient Egypt. Commodity money is also implied in our common financial term *pecuniary* (meaning "of or involving money"), which was derived from the Latin word *pecus* and originally referred to "a head of cattle."

The first coins came into use in Greece somewhere between 700 and 1000 B.C. The advantage of using coins was that their weight or volume did not have to constantly be measured out, as grain did; a coin could therefore be accepted "on sight." This characteristic undoubtedly added to the efficiency of doing business in a money economy, and thus coins became the currency of choice in the early Greek and Roman worlds. These coins were made of metal, but other cultures and communities used different forms of standardized monetary objects made out of bone, shells, baked clay, and similar materials.

Henry Lindgren, whose interest lies in the psychology of money, informs us that the Greeks first stamped their coins with the faces of their gods. It didn't take too long, however, for Greek political leaders to spread a little political propaganda by changing the faces of the gods to appear more and more like their own:

> Once Alexander was dead, all doubt about his divinity vanished. Coins bearing the head of Hercules continued to be issued in Alexander's name by local mints, but Hercules now distinctly resembled Alexander. As far as the man in the street was concerned, the face *was* that of the deified Alexander. These coins, which circulated throughout the ancient world for hundreds of years, gave visible support to the Alexander legend.[37]

Thus, not only did money help to expand trade and commerce, but it also helped to bind large and disparate communities together and to legitimize political leadership. In addition, historians have suggested that the sciences and arts of this highly civilized Greek and Roman period were, in part, byproducts of expanded money and trade and the concurrent improvement in the standard of living.

The first coins were probably commodity money consisting of gold or silver (or, in the case of the early Greek "dumps,"—

bean-shaped lumps—that were amalgams of precious metals). With the expansion of trade and the inherent limitations of mining sufficient quantities of gold and silver, the Greeks and others eventually turned to what we call **fiat money**—money that is declared by the government to have value. Such coinage becomes mere **token money,** since its metal content (usually bronze and copper) is decidedly less than the face value of the coin. Paper currency (such as our own dollars) would also be, by definition, fiat money. The Chinese are believed to have used the first paper money, which (as reported by Marco Polo) was made out of the bark of the mulberry tree.*

Returning once more to our desert island example, the banking committee now must consider whether to go with commodity money (shoelaces, buttons, etc.) or fiat money made up and issued by the committee itself. They finally decide, with great solemnity, to issue signed pieces of paper as their official money supply.

The last problem the islanders must face is how they are going to make the new currency valuable. What, in fact, makes any currency valuable? Shifting from our desert island to the U.S. economy, we might ask, "What makes our own dollar valuable?"

The U.S. Dollar

Many people are under the misconception that the government backs up the value of every dollar with a precious commodity metal, such as gold or silver. They may be surprised to discover that the last vestige of gold backing (25 cents on the dollar) was removed by Congress in 1967. Thus, the $1 or $5 bill in your pocket or wallet is unbacked fiat money.

If you check the front of a $1 bill (or any U.S. paper currency), you will see to the upper left the declaration "THIS NOTE IS LEGAL TENDER FOR ALL DEBTS, PUBLIC AND PRIVATE." This printed statement does not, however, guarantee the inherent value and spending potential of the bill. Other currencies with similar declarations have hyperinflated to the point of uselessness,

---

*I am indebted to Professor Henry Lindgren for the details in this discussion of monetary history. [See Lindgren's *Great Expectations* (Los Altos, CA: William Kaufmann, 1980).]

grossly eroding the public's faith and purchasing power. No, what makes our dollars valuable is really a matter of social trust. Money is valuable because we have faith that each one of us will accept it as a legitimate medium of exchange. If all of a sudden everyone thought that money had no value, then indeed it would have no value.

Fortunately, there is no reason for people to abandon faith in their dollars—unless, of course, the government doesn't do its job. If, for example, the government issued too much money, then money would become too plentiful, and there would be a relative shortage of things to buy. We would then experience inflation. Under extreme conditions of hyperinflation, the public could lose faith in government currency and return to bartering or develop blackmarket currencies.

On the other hand, if there is not enough money to go around, normal economic transactions would be stifled, which can also be dangerous for the economy. Just the right balance between output and money must be achieved for our dollars to remain valuable.

There was a time, however, when our citizens did not accept the legitimacy of the federal currency. The man who became our first President spoke with great fervor on this subject:

> George Washington...denounced those who refused to accept at full value the bills of the Continental Congress as "pests to society and the greatest enemies we have to the happiness of America. I would to God that some one of the more atrocious in each state was hung in gibbets upon a gallows five times as high as the one prepared by Haman.[38]

People do not put their faith and trust in a monetary system automatically; the public's faith and trust must be earned by careful monetary regulation and controls. How then is the U.S. money supply controlled? This is a good question, but one that most Americans probably would not answer correctly.

It is generally thought that our money supply is controlled simply by turning the printing presses on and off. If we want more money, the government just prints it up. This notion is only partly true, since our money supply (our assets that can be spent immediately) is more than just currency (bills and coins); it is also in the form of **demand deposits,** or checking accounts. Today, in fact, there is considerably more money in demand deposits than in total currency. Thus, to control the money supply, we must be able to regulate these demand-deposit dollars as well as the paper currency. How is this done?

Think of the billions of dollars in checking accounts throughout the United States. Much of this money must be derived from a variety of credit forms, such as mortgages, installment credit, and business credit. Thus, it is reasonable to assume that if the government could manipulate credit conditions in some way, it would have some control over the money supply. Easy credit conditions usually mean more loans; more loans, in turn, mean more dollars flowing through the economy.

Thus, if the government can control credit conditions, not only can it affect the money supply but also, perhaps more importantly, it can influence the total amount of spending. This means that whoever is in charge of the money supply (through credit manipulation) can have as much power over the economic system as those who control the federal budget. We already know that the President and Congress regulate the budget, but who is responsible for regulating credit conditions and the money supply?

The Federal Reserve System

The money supply is determined and regulated in large part by our central banking system, the **Federal Reserve System** (often simply called the Fed). In fact, if we were to pinpoint where major decisions are made on money matters, we would zero in on the seven-person Board of Governors of the Federal Reserve System in Washington, D.C. From there, we would move down to the 12 regional Federal Reserve Banks situated in major cities around the country. Take a moment to look at a $1 bill and see from which Federal Reserve Bank it was issued. (The source is written around the large letter to the left of Washington's face.) Your dollar was probably issued by a Federal Reserve Bank nearby. Three bills randomly selected from my wallet came from Minneapolis (I), St. Louis (H), and Chicago (G).

Monetary control then flows from the 12 regional Federal Reserve Banks down to the commercial banks that belong to the Federal Reserve System. These commercial banks, often called **member banks,** hold stock in the Federal Reserve System and are required to follow certain policies established by the Fed. Perhaps you know of a "First National" bank in your area; you can be sure that it is one of these member banks.

Not all banks belong to the Fed, however. Only about one third of all commercial banks are members of the system. Before 1980, this distinction was fairly important because member banks had to meet stiffer requirements that tied up money that could otherwise be earning interest. Thus, it was not surprising to see a sizable number of national banks defect from Fed membership and become state banks, so that they could, in effect, utilize more of their funds.

In this pre-1980 period, even greater distinctions were made between regular banks and other so-called "thrift" institutions, such as savings and loans (S&Ls) and credit unions. For example, an S&L was allowed to offer savers slightly higher interest returns, with the expectation that they would specialize in meeting their community's housing loan needs. They were not, however, allowed to compete with banks on several fronts, including the issuing of checking accounts. Rigid compartmentalization was the rule of the day.

All this changed during the deregulation of the Carter and Reagan administrations. Specifically, the Depository Institutions Deregulation and Monetary Control Act of 1980 phased in new policies that effectively blurred many previous distinctions. Today, as you probably know, all depository institutions can offer their customers some type of checking (demand-deposit) account. In return for this privilege, these institutions adhere to many of the same rules that member banks follow, including the same reserve requirements; this, in turn, helps the Federal Reserve to maintain its broad-based control of the credit system. Putting it another way, the Deregulation Act of 1980 created a competitive free-for-all that essentially made all financial institutions rivals for essentially the same business. How then do these banks and thrift institutions make their profits?

The profit philosophy is actually quite simple: "Borrow money cheap; lend it dear." The difference between the rate of interest paid out for saving, checking, and other depositor accounts and the rate of interest charged for mortgage, installment, and business loans is the primary source of industry profits. Thus, the major responsibility of commercial banks and thrift institutions is to take in the deposits from those who want to save and to lend out that money to those who want to borrow. These institutions are what economists call **financial interme-diaries**—the middle operators between savers and investors.

If commercial banks and thrift institutions hold deposits and make loans, then what do regional Federal Reserve Banks do? Each regional bank is a kind of banker's bank; it also holds deposits and makes loans. The deposits are called **reserves** (hence, Federal Reserve), and the loans are called **discounts.** The regional reserve banks also function as clearinghouses for the millions and millions of checks sent around the country, and they supervise the member banks in their region. Finally, the 12 regional Federal Reserve Banks supply their districts with Federal Reserve Notes (the commonly used paper currency in our wallets).

However, the real power within the Federal Reserve System—the power to influence credit and spending and, ultimately, unemployment and inflation—rests with the Board of Governors and its various committees. How does the Board influence the money supply, and what mysterious tools does this small band of government bankers have at its command?

We learned earlier in this chapter that the key to influencing the money supply is the control of credit. Therefore, when the Fed makes it difficult for the commercial banking system to give out loans, the growth of the money supply should slow down. When loans are easy to obtain, the money supply should grow at a faster rate. But how can the loan decisions of individual financial officers throughout the country be regulated? To see how this is done, we must return to the concept of reserves.

Every bank and every other depository institution must set aside a certain percentage of its deposits in the form of reserves. For example, Federal Reserve guidelines might say that your local bank must set aside at least 12 percent of its total demand deposits (assets in checking accounts). We call this percentage the **reserve ratio.** Let's look at an example to see how this works.

Suppose that you live in Central City, New York, and that your newly established commercial bank has an initial deposit of $1,000 in demand deposits. If the reserve ratio for checking accounts is 12 percent, then your bank must set aside a reserve of $120. However, the directors of the Central City First National Bank might decide that if they want to make any loans, they should maintain some excess reserves above and beyond the required $120. Do you see why?

If any customers borrow money from the Central City bank and then cash their loan checks at another bank, Central City would lose those reserves and the other bank would gain them. Assume that our bank (with only $120 in reserves) just loans Sarah Smith $500, which she immediately deposits in her checking account. If Sarah later decides to take the full $500 and spend it all out of state while vacationing in Florida, then the Central City bank won't have sufficient funds to transfer to the Florida bank. (Remember that all payments between banks involve a transfer of reserves.) Therefore, to safely loan Sarah the $500, Central City bank would be wise to have at least $500 in excess reserves to cover the loan.

In summary, *a bank's capacity to lend out money depends primarily on the size of its excess reserves.* When large amounts of excess reserves are generally distributed throughout the country, we usually find easy money conditions; if commercial banks around the country are holding few excess reserves, we can expect tight money conditions. We should also note that when "new" dollars are loaned out (and "new" money is created), other banks receive this additional money. These banks can, in turn, use this money (after holding the required fraction of reserves) to further expand the money supply—in a way similar to the multiplier effect we examined in Chapter 8. Naturally, this monetary multiplier works in reverse if there is a net reduction in commercial loans.

Monetary Policy

The obvious question we must now ask is, "Since the key to controlling credit conditions and the money supply lies in controlling excess reserves, exactly how does the Federal Reserve influence the amount of excess reserves in the banking system?"

One way is simply by raising or lowering the reserve ratio. To use an exaggerated example, what would happen if the Fed increased the reserve ratio from 12 to 20 percent? The excess reserves of all U.S. commercial lending institutions would suddenly be diminished by billions and billions of dollars, and credit would become tight. On the other hand, if the Fed lowered the reserve ratio requirement, then the excess reserves of all depository institutions would automatically expand, and credit conditions would ease up. Power over the reserve ratio therefore translates into power over the money supply.

Another monetary tool the Fed uses to manipulate excess reserves is the buying and selling of government securities, called **open-market operations.** U.S. commercial banks presently hold billions of dollars worth of government obligations in the form of bonds, notes, and other securities. Banks purchase these securities because the government frequently offers them at attractive interest rates. To reduce excess reserves, all the Fed has to do is sell more securities to the member banks. This reduction comes about because banks pay for the securities by taking the money out of their reserve accounts. The immediate lowering of these reserves thus reduces the potential loaning capacity of the commercial banks, tightening money conditions throughout the economy.

If, instead, the Fed decides to buy securities from commercial banks, then the process is reversed. The money from the Fed will enlarge the reserve accounts of the banks, and more potential money will be available for customer loans. Buying back securities from the banks may therefore result in more loans, an increase in the money supply, and (it is hoped) more spending.

The specific group that decides whether to buy or sell government securities to member banks is the **Open Market Committee.** It should be noted that open-market operations are used more frequently than the manipulation of the reserve ratio. When the Fed changes the reserve ratio—particularly upward—it causes great hardships for banks that are "all loaned up," or have already lent out their maximum amounts of money. The flexibility and ease of the open-market operation make it the number one monetary tool used by the Federal Reserve.

Our last major monetary control is called the **discount rate.** Remember from our earlier discussion that one of the Fed's services to member banks and other depository institutions is a borrowing privilege. These loans are discounts, and the interest rate on these loans is the discount rate. By raising the discount rate, the Fed discourages borrowing. Banks that reduce the amount of money they borrow from the Fed will have less money to lend out to their own customers.

On the other hand, lowering the discount rate encourages some bank borrowing; these banks will then have more excess reserves to meet the local demand for mortgages, installment loans, etc. Lowering the discount rate can also indirectly influence other interest rates throughout the economy. For example, when the discount rate is lowered, most banks are inclined to return the favor by lowering interest rates on their own loans.

These three controls—the reserve ratio, open-market operations, and the discount rate—are the monetary tools that the Fed uses not only to regulate the money supply but also to help stabilize the economy.

Now let's summarize what we learned about monetary policies and apply that to what we already know about supply and demand. First, we consider inflation. If our country were facing severe inflation, the Fed would probably do one, two, or all of the following:

1. Raise the reserve ratio.
2. Raise the discount rate.
3. Sell government securities.

This monetary policy leads to:

less excess reserves
↓
less commercial loans
↓
less money
↓
higher interest rates

If money becomes very scarce, overall interest rates can go sky high, as they did in 1970, 1974, and the early 1980s. The combined impact of high interest rates and tight money conditions usually discourages business investment spending and dampens consumer demand for interest-sensitive durables, such as automobiles and housing. This sequence of events ultimately leads to a reduction in investment spending and is the basis of the Fed's anti-inflationary monetary policies.

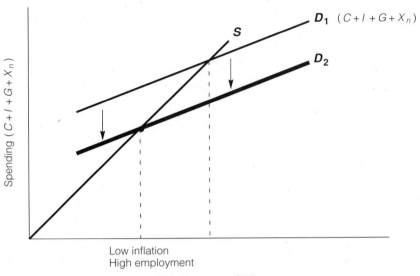

FIGURE 9-1 If the economy experiences high inflation due to excess demand (D_1), then the Federal Reserve can undertake anti-inflationary monetary policies to lower demand to a noninflationary level of GDP (D_2).

We have come full circle. Our economic controls for influencing spending are now complete.

Recall our graphs of total supply and total demand in Figures 8-6, 8-7, and 8-8. There, we described the Keynesian fiscal policies that could raise or lower consumption spending C through changes in taxes and government spending G. The total demand curve may rise or fall, depending on whether we are facing inflation or recession.

Now we know that monetary policies also have a profound impact on a third important component of total spending—investment spending I. Monetary policies that combat inflation will therefore affect our graph of total supply and total demand as shown in Figure 9-1. Now, what about a *recession?*

In a recession, the appropriate monetary policies for easing credit would be:

1. Lower the reserve ratio.

2. Lower the discount rate.

3. Buy government securities.

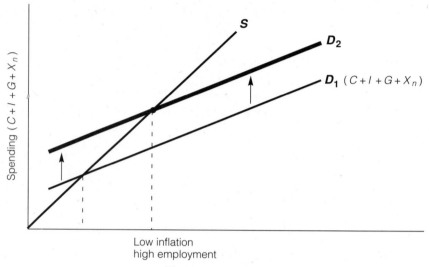

FIGURE 9-2 If the economy is sluggish as a result of too little demand (D_1), then the Federal Reserve can undertake *anti-recessionary* monetary policies to stimulate investment spending I, thereby expanding aggregate demand to D_2.

In theory, then, excess reserves will increase first. Then, as the money supply grows, credit will be easier to obtain. More money in the system will eventually drive interest rates down. Easier money and low interest rates should encourage investment spending, which, in turn, will help to lift up the total demand curve (see Figure 9-2).

How closely do these theories match reality? Economists are quick to point out that monetary policies are more effective in combating inflation than recession. During an inflationary period, the monetary screw can be tightened until money and credit are actually squeezed off. In 1970 and again in 1981, we experienced some of the harmful side effects of ultratight money—for example, a depression in the housing industry when mortgage rates were driven to unreasonable levels.

On the other hand, lowering interest rates and making credit easily available does not force businesses to increase investments. During the Great Depression, for example, interest rates were very low, but the other negative factors—the stock market slump, low incomes, loss of confidence, and general pessimism—far outweighed the expansionary effects of easy money. More recently, in the 1990–91 slump, the Federal Reserve forced a large drop in interest rates. The Fed's discount rate, for example, went from 7 percent (Jan. 1991) down to a 25-year low of 3.5 percent by the end of 1991. But again, general pessimism, debt repayment worries, and fears over job security diluted the full impact of the policy. Still the low rates did help set the stage for an eventual recovery.

Thus we might say that the Federal Reserve is currently in a Keynesian mode, where the Board of Governors is, in effect, making a conscious effort to adjust credit conditions, the money supply, and interest rates to correct problems in the U.S. economy. This interventionist approach has also been referred to as **discretionary monetary policy.**

Paul Hellman, writing for *The Wall Street Journal's* editorial page, has some fun with Fed Chairman Alan Greenspan's incessant tinkering with the economy—adjusting this, adjusting that—as if he (or his Fed Board) were playing the metaphoric role of auto mechanic:

> The Fed sometimes must roll up its sleeves and adjust the economic machinery. The Fed spends a lot of time either tightening things or loosening things, or debating about whether to tighten or loosen. Imagine a customer taking his car into Greenspan's Garage.
>
> > Normally calm, Skeezik Greenspan took one look at the car and started to sweat. This would be hard to fix—it was an economy car: "What's the problem?" asked Greenspan.
> >
> > "It's been running beautifully for over six years now," said the customer. "But recently it's been acting sluggish."
> >
> > "These cars are tricky," said Greenspan. "We can always loosen a few screws, as long as you don't mind the side effects."
> >
> > "What side effects?" asked the customer.
> >
> > "Nothing at first," said Greenspan. "We won't even know if the repairs have worked for at least a year. After that, either everything will be fine, or your car will accelerate wildly and go totally out of control."
> >
> > "Just as long as it doesn't stall," said the customer. "I hate that."[39]

All humor aside, this description does tend to approximate the school of thought that our economy needs an activist Federal Reserve. It should be noted, however, that there is a group of economists who feel that this tinkering (sometimes called fine-tuning) creates more problems than it solves. They call themselves **monetarists** and include, among others, Milton Friedman and Allan Meltzer. Let's take a brief look at some of their arguments and suggestions.

Monetarism

Inherent in the **monetarist philosophy** is a distinct distrust of government in general and a specific distrust of the government's ability to know enough about current and future economic conditions to time its interventionist policies accurately to stabilize the business cycle. Friedman, for one, has looked at the historical data of monetary growth versus economic performance and concluded that the Fed's tendency toward frequent intervention has actually been counterproductive: Fed policies—undertaken in good faith—have produced even greater, not lesser, swings in the business cycle, according to Friedman.

For monetarists, money indeed matters; it is the chief determinant of current macroeconomic problems. On the other hand, money has the potential to contribute to macroeconomic solutions. The way to achieve economic stability, as the monetarist sees it, is by a simple **monetary rule:** increase the money supply at a relatively constant rate month after month, year after year.

Friedman advocates an increase of 3 to 5 percent per year— an expansion in the money supply commensurate with the potential long-run growth rate of overall economic activity. Surges in money growth will, according to Friedman, eventually result in inflation; discretionary cuts, after a time lag, will move the economy toward recession. Given the monetarist's strict 3 to 5 percent rule, we would no longer use a heroic metaphor for the role of the Federal Reserve Chairman (even Hellman's auto mechanic would be inappropriate). According to the monetarist view, stable money growth creates the optimal conditions for long-run economic success—like a robotic dispenser feeding monetary nourishment on a predictable and steady basis to a healthy, growing economy.

In conclusion, whatever role the Fed takes or the dilemmas it faces, today or in the future, it will nonetheless continue to be a critical economic institution—hopefully one that helps to maintain a stable economy, a healthy financial system, and most importantly, a trustworthy monetary base from which we can all go about our private economic affairs with a feeling of confidence.

Questions for Thought and Discussion

1. Should a tight monetary policy or an easy monetary policy be used during stagflation?
2. A variety of events, including thrift deregulation and tax laws that encouraged risky real estate investments (plus some outright fraud and financial mismanagement) has created the so-called "Savings & Loan Crisis" which, according to estimates, may cost the U.S. taxpayer somewhere between $300 billion and $500 billion. Question: How healthy are the S&Ls in your home town? Also, outline your own approach to solving the crisis that combines economic efficiency, fairness, and also takes into account current political realities.
3. Could blades of grass be used as money? Why or why not?
4. True or false? The only way for a monetary system to work is for each unit of money (dollar, pound, yen, franc, etc.) to be backed by gold or silver equal to the value of that unit of money. Explain.

— NEW PERSPECTIVES —

Mysteries of the Dollar . . . The Great Seal

Have you ever inspected a dollar bill, especially the side with the great seal (circles containing the eagle and the pyramid)? Undoubtedly you have glanced at it now and then. Why not pull out a bill right now and take another look. You may first be puzzled, then intrigued as to what the various images mean.

What we see in the right circle is, of course, our national bird, the bald eagle. The ribbon in his beak contains the Latin words *E Pluribus Unum,* translated: "Out of the many, one." Also look carefully at what the eagle is grasping. In one talon are thirteen arrows. (Why thirteen?) These arrows represent the principle of national defense. However, clasped in its other talon, we see a laurel

(continued)

branch, a softer symbol representing life and peaceful coexistence. There is little doubt as to the preferred course for the nation. (Indeed, it's no accident that the eagle was drawn facing which of the two sides?) Above the eagle is a cloud (or ring) of light—sometimes called a "glory." How many stars in the cloud?

Now, what about that mysterious pyramid? It's not certain, but historians think that it was Thomas Jefferson who suggested that we incorporate Egyptian symbolism in our great seal. Here, the key number is *three;* i.e., three angles of the pyramidal shape:

> The three visible angles of the pyramid were designed to symbolize political, economic, and spiritual freedom—the three interdependent liberties in this "new order"*

The new order reference is in the lower inscription, *Norvus Ordo Seclorum,* or "New order of the ages"; a boast that, for this new nation at least, history will be starting afresh. In back of the pyramid is a desert (the effete old order) and in front (look carefully), you will see tiny sproutings symbolizing the fertility and unlimited possibilities of this new land. The pyramid itself, like the infant nation, is unfinished. Mythologist Joseph Campbell wrote that the floating eye is the "Eye of the Holy Spirit," not so much the god of our religious faith but the power of the rational mind:

> Mankind has herewith come of age and taken to itself responsibility and authority for shaping of human lives according to Reason.**

And the words *Annuit Coeptis?* This translates into "He (or it) smiles on our beginnings," which when combined with the eye, conveys a comforting thought that something good is brewing here at the birth of a new nation.

Question: Comment on the appropriateness of the dollar's mottos and symbolism. Specifically, what is meant by "Out of the many, one?" If you were asked to redesign the great seal, would you try something new? If so, what would you change? If you have the chance, check out the currency from a different country (try a coin and stamp shop). Contrast their mottos and symbols with those on the American dollar.

* Tregarthen, Suzanne. "The U.S. Dollar Symbolizes Political, Economic and Spiritual Freedom." *The Margin* (Boulder, CO), Spring, 1992: p. 54.
** Campbell, Joseph. *The Inner Reaches of Outer Space.* New York: Harper & Row, 1988, p. 126.

10

The Benefits of Trade

It has become commonplace to hear businesspeople, economists, and government officials speak of a global economy. They proclaim that our jobs, our markets—indeed, our very material comforts—are becoming more and more dependent on international economic arrangements. Representative of this reality is the emergence of world **multinational** corporations, which take advantage of business opportunities with minimal regard for, or loyalty to, their country of origin. Consider, for example, the following press release:

> General Motors Corp. is going to put a French name on a German car that will be built in South Korea for export to America. GM's Pontiac division will resurrect the Le Mans name and put it on the subcompact economy car. The car was designed by GM's West German subsidiary, Adam Opel AC, and will be built by Daewoo Group Ltd., which is 50 percent owned by GM.[40]

At the root of these changes is, of course, a growing desire among nations to engage in international trade. Perhaps it is time to explore some very basic questions in economics that reflect this expanding global reality: "Why do countries like the United States, Japan, Mexico, Germany, and Canada trade? What's in it for them? What's in it for us? How do we benefit?" Let's examine some possible answers.

Why Is Trade Necessary?

The most obvious reason to trade is to get essential or highly desirable raw materials that cannot be obtained domestically. For example, the United States must import most of its bauxite (for use in aluminum smelting), chromium, manganese, cobalt, and, to a lesser extent, oil, potash (for use in fertilizers), zinc, nickel, and tin. Add to this list some nonessential (but desirable) food imports, such as coffee, tea, bananas, and cocoa, and you can begin to see how important international trade is to the United States. And what is true for our nation is even more true for countries that are less endowed with the basic raw materials of industrial production.

Another reason to trade is to promote competition in highly concentrated oligopolistic industries. Consumers almost always benefit from having a greater choice of products. Imported products frequently offer American consumers more variety and better quality at lower prices. Of course, this kind of international rivalry may annoy or even hurt some domestic industries. In the end, however, healthy competition and a greater degree of consumer choice usually improve standards of living.

Also remember that trade is a two-way street: it benefits the exporting industries as well as the importing industries. Consumers and businesses in foreign countries purchase tremendous quantities of American agricultural commodities, as well as many products manufactured in the United States, including computers, plastics, farm machinery, paper products, chemicals, medical technology, and aircraft. When discussing the pros and cons of trade, we should not forget that approximately one out of every eight American jobs depends on healthy trade arrangements with the rest of the world.

International trade also creates a sense of interdependence among world nations and can have the side effect of enhancing world peace. "We need you, and you need us" is the unspoken theme, as a continuous flow of imports and exports ties countries together with invisible threads of mutual benefits and often enhanced mutual trust. Free trade among the formerly antagonistic Common Market countries (primarily Germany, Britain, France, Italy) provides a good example. The binding effect of trade, however, is sometimes no match for the explosive forces of nationalism. During the 1979 anti-Western revolution in Iran, for example, the mutual benefits of foreign trade did not overcome a deep-seated Iranian hostility toward, and mistrust of, the United States and others, despite the mutual benefits of trade.

Some critics of international trade feel that mutual interdependence may create an unhealthy dependence on critical imports, particularly defense-related goods and services. This problem is compounded when the essential import is controlled by a monopolistic country (the sole supplier) or, in the case of oil, by a cartel (OPEC). Thus, the huge increase in oil prices during the 1970s alerted Americans to the need to promote conservation and to develop alternative energy supplies. Keep in mind, however, that such situations are unusual and should not distract us from recognizing the overall benefits of free trade.

Perhaps you are still not convinced. The following thoughts could still be running through your mind: "Sure, trade is a good outlet for our own surpluses, and it does provide us with some essential raw materials. It may even create some healthy rivalry in certain industries. But if our nation is good at producing certain products, yet, over time, finds itself losing out to imported substitutes at the expense of domestic jobs, then how can free trade be favorable for the United States?"

This question is often on the minds of workers, business owners and managers, and elected representatives. The answer, surprisingly, is that free trade is still a positive economic influence in the long run, even though it may create punishing short-run dislocations. British economist David Ricardo made this discovery about 150 years ago when he began to question the benefits of the growing volume of trade between his home country and nearby Portugal. Ricardo observed that even though both Britain and Portugal were relatively good producers of wine and cloth, each country began to specialize in the production of one of these products over time, resulting in short-run unemployment in the respective weaker industry. Ricardo felt that both countries were better off as a result of this free-trade arrangement and set out to prove his intuitive judgment. Out of observations and analyses came Ricardo's famous **theory of comparative advantage.** Let's take a closer look at this startling economic principle.

The Theory of Comparative Advantage

Let's see how Ricardo's theory might pertain to trade between Japan and the United States. Instead of wine and cloth, we'll use television sets and rice. We know that Japan is quite good at manufacturing TVs because Japanese labor is relatively inexpensive, but it may come as a surprise that the United States is quite efficient at producing rice due to its relatively abundant land and farm-capital resources. In fact, rice is a major U.S. food export.

Let's assume that both Japan and the United States have the capability to produce both products (which they do). We can even assume that Japan has a slight edge—an **absolute advantage**—in terms of the prices of both products. Even under these conditions, however, we will see that both countries will still benefit from specialization.

To determine which product each country should produce, we must examine a simplified version of each country's **production possibilities curve** (remember the old guns-and-butter curve in Figure 1-1?). Figure 10-1 shows straight-line production possibilities curves for television sets and rice in both countries.

First, let's look at the United States. Notice that the domestic trade-off is 1 for 1: if the United States wants to produce 1 additional ton of rice, it must give up 1 TV set. For Japan, in contrast, the trade-off is 1 for 2: if Japan wants to produce 1 additional ton of rice, it must give up 2 TV sets. Even though each country is capable of producing both products, their **opportunity costs** are significantly different. For example, we can say that rice is relatively cheap in the United States (costing only 1 TV set), whereas TV sets are cheap in Japan (costing only 1/2 ton of rice). If David Ricardo were looking at these trade-offs, he would say that the United States has a **comparative advantage** in the production of rice.

Now it should be obvious that each country has something to gain from producing its own specialty product and trading it with the other country. Looking first at Japan, wouldn't Japan jump at the opportunity to trade 2 TVs to the United States and receive 2 tons of rice in return? Recall that before trade, these 2 TVs would be worth only 1 ton of rice domestically. Similarly, the United States, envious of the terms of Japanese domestic trade, would jump at the opportunity to trade 1 U.S. ton of rice

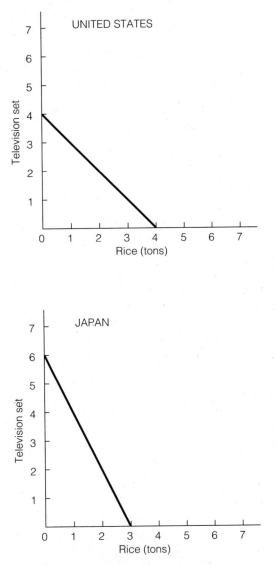

Figure 10-1 Straight-line production possibilities curves for the United States and Japan show the trade-off (or *domestic terms of trade*) between television sets and rice. For example, in the United States, the trade-off would be 4 TVs for 4 tons of rice (or 1 TV for 1 ton of rice); in Japan, the trade-off would be 6 TVs for 3 tons of rice (or 2 TVs for 1 ton of rice).

to Japan and receive 2 TVs in return—a much better deal than the 1-for-1 U.S. trade-off. But now you may be wondering, "Is there something wrong here? Exactly what advantage is there to having each country make exchanges on the basis of its own internal trade-off ratios? What's in it for the United States if, for example, it gives Japan the same terms of trade (1 for 1) that it can get for itself without trade, and vice versa?"

Ricardo would probably suggest, "Why not compromise with an international term of trade—something between 1 for 1 and 1 for 2." A likely candidate for the compromise (depending on the demand for each product) might be 1 ton of rice for 1.5 TV sets (or the equivalent ratio of 2 tons of rice for 3 TVs). Now the United States can trade 2 tons of rice for 3 TVs (better than 1 for 1!); Japan, in turn, only has to give up 3 TV sets (instead of 4) to receive 2 tons of rice.

We'll assume that both countries find this compromise satisfactory, which, as we shall see, will bring about some very positive end results. For example, the United States now has the potential to increase its total TV consumption by 50 percent; in Figure 10-1, note that if the United States wants to export all of its rice (4 tons), it can import as many as 6 TV sets. Japan's total rice potential has increased by 33 percent: if Japan exports all of its 6 TVs, it can receive as much as 4 tons of rice, instead of the original 3. These new trade possibilities can be shown on an *expanded production possibilities curve* for each country (see Figure 10-2).

These expanded production possibilities curves indicate that the consumers in each country have the opportunity to enjoy more of both products. On the average, their standards of living have improved but not due to an enlargement of either resource base; each country is simply using its original resources more efficiently by specializing in the area in which it has a comparative advantage.

According to David Ricardo, free trade gives countries this unexpected bonus. Therefore, he was not saddened when he saw the cloth industry in Britain grow at the expense of its wine industry and the cloth industry in Portugal decline as its wine production expanded. Although these trade-offs certainly caused short-run economic dislocations (unemployment, bankruptcies, etc.), the net long-run change was positive.

Actually, the benefits of international trade are really no different than the benefits of local or regional trade. Think, for example, about the obvious advantages of trade within the United States. There is a significant difference, however, between international trade and domestic trade: the dislocations

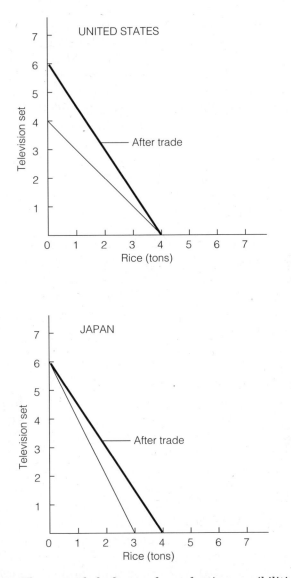

Figure 10-2 The expanded after-trade production possibilities curves for the United States and Japan imply that specialization and trade based on comparative advantage provide higher standards of living in both countries.

caused by foreign imports are usually more abrasive politically than the dislocations caused by purely domestic trade. This issue, in turn, brings us to the heart of an important and sensitive subject—**protectionism.**

Trade Protectionism

One of the best ways to illustrate the pressures to restrict imports (without losing sight of the benefits of trade) is to draw up an exaggerated example of trade between two states. Imagine that a particular state—say, Wisconsin—is actually a small, self-reliant country, producing most (if not all) of its essential economic requirements. We'll further assume that the people of Wisconsin have an unusual craving for citrus fruits and that, over the years, a thriving orange and grapefruit industry has grown up in this country.

At this point, you might be wondering, "How could Wisconsin, way up there along the northern U.S. border, grow citrus fruit?" The answer is that if the domestic demand is great enough (if the people of Wisconsin are willing and able to pay high prices for citrus fruit), then it will be profitable to grow oranges and grapefruit in artificially heated hothouses. Let's say that fruit grown under these conditions will be priced at $3 for an orange and $4 for a grapefruit.

Now assume that once Wisconsin establishes its large and thriving citrus industry, some enterprising individual discovers that the "country" of Florida can grow an orange for $0.10 and a grapefruit for $0.15. Adding another $0.05 for shipping, our entrepreneurial friend finds that he can make a good profit selling these fruits in Wisconsin at a fraction of the industry prices there.

It does not take any imagination to guess what will happen after the cheap Florida imports began to roll into Wisconsin. First, there is shock and dismay among the domestic (Wisconsin) citrus growers. Horror stories circulate, resulting in corporate bankruptcies, loss of tax revenues, and long unemployment lines. A powerful trade association, the Wisconsin Citrus Growers Association (WCGA), is formed and immediately begins to exert political pressure to help save the Wisconsin citrus industry. Soon the political machinery begins to respond, undertaking measures to promote Wisconsin fruit consumption and to discourage the importation of Florida fruit.

The first measures take the form of **nontariff barriers,** subtle methods of dealing with the import problem without resorting to the more common tariffs and quotas. First, massive advertising campaigns praise the virtues of domestically grown fruit and might imply that some of the cheap Florida imports have been determined to be unhealthy. We'll assume, however, that the Wisconsin consumer finds the imported fruit just as tasty and wholesome as the home grown variety. The next tactic is to pass a law stating that all imported fruit must be dyed blue. But even that strategy doesn't work—the price is too good!

Sooner or later, the Wisconsin growers convince their legislators to take more drastic steps, such as setting tariffs and quotas. We will examine these measures in greater detail, but first let's take a look at what we have learned about the real world from this example.

The first lesson is that cheap imported products almost always cause some economic dislocation in directly affected industries. Assertions of comparative advantage are not very comforting to workers who have lost their livelihoods and incomes. Their first reaction is almost always shock, followed by intense anger. Consider the following story from a St. Paul, Minnesota, newspaper:

> Workers at the Teledyne Wisconsin Motor firm, which was playing host to Japanese businessmen, hauled down a Japanese flag in front of the plant and raised an American flag on the same pole.
>
> They sang the "Star Spangled Banner" as the American banner was raised.
>
> One worker tried to burn the Japanese flag but could not ignite it. He then slashed it with a pocket knife, took it across the street, and shoved it down a sewer opening.
>
> John Claffey, president of Local 283 of the United Auto Workers, said . . . the transfer of the so-called Wisconsin Robin engine business to Japan had cost "50 percent of our engine business" and the 350 people had been laid off at the West Milwaukee plant as a result.[41]

These intense feelings are understandable. Compassion tells us that workers who are adversely affected by sudden shifts in international trade arrangements need help to offset the pain of sudden unemployment and to shift their skills and resources to new industries in which they do have a comparative advantage.

This point brings us to the second real-world lesson in our illustration. It should be clear that despite the economic hardship, Wisconsin really has no business growing grapefruit and oranges. Its land, resources, and climate are far more ideal for producing dairy products. Once Wisconsin begins to specialize and to trade dairy products for inexpensive Florida citrus fruit,

Hi. I used to own the largest orange-growing hot house complex in Wisconsin. We grew our oranges even during the harshest Wisconsin winters. Sure they weren't cheap because of high fuel costs. But they sure tasted great!

DAVE'S ORANGES
WISCONSIN GROWN
HEATING PLANT

One day my neighbor Chester Olson, Jr., came back from a vacation in Florida with a load of oranges which sold for a tenth as much as mine. He sold out in hours, then went back to get more. Well that got us Wisconsin orange growers thinking. Soon we had a law passed that required all Florida oranges to be dyed blue.

ANNUAL ORANGE GROWERS OF WISCONSIN CONVENTION
CHESTER
Proposed NEW LAW All Florida oranges must be Dyed Blue
PETITIONS

We did this for our customers' convenience, err...that way they wouldn't accidentally buy inferior Florida oranges. Well that didn't help too much, so we tried to reduce our costs by putting cows in our hot houses (the cows seemed to generate quite a bit of heat).

Even that didn't help our orange business. Then one day Chester, Jr., came by asking if he couldn't buy some of my milk to take back to Florida. He says milk there costs $10 a gallon while I can sell it to him for a dollar a gallon. Hmmm, maybe I really ought to be producing milk instead of oranges.

Hmm?
CHESTER INC.

Sure enough, my cows were producing milk cheaper here in Wisconsin because they seem to like the cooler Wisconsin weather and our rolling pastures. This makes it possible to ship my cheap milk to Florida. By the way, those inexpensive Florida oranges aren't really that bad after all.

FLORIDA ORANGES
FLORIDA

Well that's about it. I'm now a prosperous Wisconsin dairy farmer. One thing I wonder about though...why does Florida make me dye my milk green?

KV

both Wisconsin and Florida will enjoy higher standards of living compared with the days before trade.

Thus, the most productive reaction to the import threat is for Wisconsin to start promoting a dairy industry. To facilitate this change, the government may have to offer temporary, low-cost loans for certain types of farm investments, set up research facilities, and help to seek out potential markets for dairy products. Indeed, it would be economically disastrous to hold on to citrus production at all costs. Such a reaction would lock Wisconsin's resources into the wrong industry for years and years.

Strong protectionist reflexes are, however, far more common than attempts to adjust to new economic realities. We therefore need to take a closer look at the nature of these restrictions to see how they work and how they affect the consumer.

Tariffs and Quotas

Certainly, the most common strategy for discouraging imports is to levy **tariffs**—taxes on specific imported goods. Although tariffs are sometimes justified by the claim that they will generate tax revenues, their real intent is almost always to choke off foreign competition. Indeed, if revenues were the issue, there would be no point in specifically discriminating against foreign manufacturers and levying such taxes just on them.

The economic effect of a tariff is the same as that of an excise tax on any product: it lifts the supply curve precisely by the amount of the tax. The degree to which this hurts the consumer depends on *demand elasticity*. Figure 10-3a shows a fairly elastic demand for Mexican tomatoes; Figure 10-3b illustrates an inelastic demand for Canadian natural gas. In each case, the supply curve has moved a vertical distance equal to the amount of the tariff ($0.50 per unit). But due to the different demand elasticities, the tariff on the tomatoes increases the final price to the consumer only slightly while the same tariff on natural gas translates into a large price increase. The explanation for this can be traced to the fact that imported tomatoes are a non-necessity; several other vegetables can be substituted for tomatoes. Natural gas, however, is a necessity that has few substitutes. The consumer, therefore, has little or no choice but to absorb most of the $0.50 tariff.

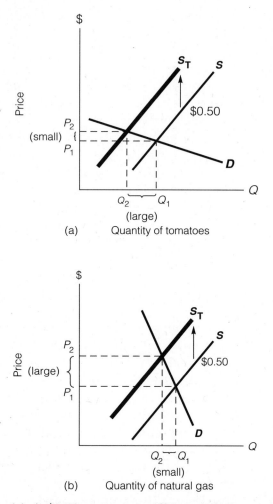

FIGURE 10-3 (a) A $0.50 per-unit tariff imposed on a product with a relatively elastic demand raises the import price slightly but curtails the quantity demanded by a large amount. (b) The same $0.50 per-unit tariff levied on a product with an inelastic demand raises the import price considerably but has little impact on the quantity demanded.

Perhaps of even greater concern to the domestic industry, which pushed for the tariff in the first place, is how the tariff affects the quantity demanded of an import. The choking-off effect on imports is obviously greater in the elastic tomato market than in the inelastic natural gas market. Generally speaking, we can say that the greater the demand elasticity, the more a tariff will help the domestic industry achieve its goal of keeping out foreign competition.

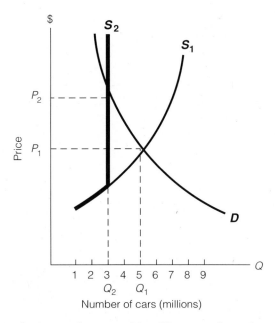

FIGURE 10-4   An imposed quota of 3 million cars fixes the supply curve in a vertical position at S_2 directly above the quota quantity. The equilibrium price after the quota is P_2. (Note that the free-market equilibrium price is P_1.)

When the tariff is not effective, however, a second, more extreme protectionist strategy, the import **quota,** can be used. Quotas simply limit the quantities of imports that are legally allowed to enter the country, so that cheap goods will not flood the domestic market. The impact of a quota can be seen in Figure 10-4.

Although economists do not favor any form of protectionist measure, they may dislike quotas most of all. At least with a tariff, it is possible to obtain an additional quantity of a product if the consumer is willing to pay the tax. But the quota is an *absolute barrier* once the legal limit has been reached. In Figure 10-4, the foreign quota was set at 3 million cars, but the normal trade equilibrium would have been 5 million cars. Also note that the restricted S_2 supply forces consumers who want to purchase the product to bid the price up from P_1 to P_2. When faced with quotas, some exporters simply upgrade their exported product by selling only the most expensive (and therefore most profitable) units, unfairly shutting out many lower-income families from the benefits of trade.

Indeed, if there is one thread running throughout this discussion, it is that protectionist measures usually hurt all types of consumers and ultimately diminish the efficient use of world resources. Yet they are still enforced. A major reason is the political influence of the workers and businesses affected by foreign competition (recall the Wisconsin citrus growers example). However, it is sometimes difficult to understand why the public itself supports trade restrictions. Let's examine some of the arguments most frequently offered by both the vested interest groups and the general public.

Arguments for Trade Protectionism

A student once said (quite sincerely) that we ought to restrict foreign imports because it's important "to keep our money in our country." This argument has an irrefutable ring to it: how could we not want to keep our dollars at home?

On further reflection, however, this is actually a counterproductive argument. Again, we should recognize that trade is a two-way street. For example, U.S. dollars that go to Japan for VCRs or Toyotas come back to our country when the Japanese buy our rice, soybeans, stocks and bonds, computers, and real estate, or help to finance our public debt by purchasing securities from the U.S. Treasury. If there is a healthy trade arrangement between these two countries, our money will eventually return to us because the Japanese have no need to hold on to U.S. dollars at home.

Another argument we hear quite often is that our country ought to restrict imports because our workers cannot compete with cheap foreign labor. This powerful, often emotionally charged issue—the claim that products from low-wage countries jeopardize American wage rates, American businesses, and, ultimately, American jobs—should not be dismissed lightly.

Proponents of this argument often overlook the fact that U.S. wages are higher than wages in other countries, primarily because U.S. workers are generally more productive, better educated, and more skilled. Often, American workers also use more advanced production techniques than foreign workers do. In fact, other less technologically advanced countries have sometimes argued for tariffs to protect their domestic industries from the unfair competition of the highly productive American industrial worker or farmer. In certain industries, of course, U.S. wage rates may be out of line with industry's general level of worker productivity. But why should the American consumer be forced, through protectionist import restrictions, to subsidize high U.S. wage rates that are not matched by corresponding productivity? Or, putting it slightly differently, why shouldn't U.S. consumers be allowed to benefit from inexpensive products made by low-wage workers? And, equally importantly, why shouldn't foreign consumers benefit from the output of our nation's most efficient industries?

If you scratch beneath the surface of the cheap foreign labor argument, you usually discover that it is an oblique admission that a particular U.S. industry is no longer efficient according to world standards. In certain cases, some of the producers may not have modernized their factories; in other industries, wages may be out of line with productivity or product design or quality may not have kept up with foreign competition. Indeed, it would be unusual if we didn't see some domestic industries (or individual companies) lose their competitive advantages over time.

Needless to say, if we begin to erect trade barriers based on the cheap foreign labor argument, there is no reason why other countries cannot retaliate with their own tariffs and quotas on U.S. producers. This would be the beginning of a destructive **trade-restriction war** where everybody would lose in the end. A good illustration of such shortsightedness, the enactment of the Smoot-Hawley tariffs in 1930 raised the average cost of goods imported to the United States by about 60 percent. Foreign retaliation ensued, and the inevitable cutback in world trade made the Great Depression of the 1930s just that much worse.

The popularity of such seemingly "logical" arguments should not mask the fact that they simply do not hold up under scrutiny. But perhaps you're wondering, "Are there any conditions under which interference with free trade might be warranted?" The answer to this question is a qualified maybe.

When a country is confronted with a violation of international morality, restrictions on both imports and exports may be justified on *ethical grounds*. The United States, for example, has, in the past, put trade restrictions on South Africa for their undemocratic, apartheid policies. In the late 1970s, President Jimmy Carter placed an embargo on grain exports to the Soviet Union after their invasion of Afghanistan; and, more recently, a United Nations sanctioned trade embargo was placed on Iraq after the Gulf War in 1991, in response to the continuation of Saddam Hussein's repressive actions and policies.

It has been argued that Third World countries should temporarily restrict imports to give their new domestic industries an opportunity to become established. This is usually referred to as the **infant industry argument.** Its implications are that (1) it is desirable for less-developed countries to diversify their internal economies, and (2) temporary restrictions are needed so that the infant can have breathing space to mature, to become efficient by world standards, without getting unduly hurt by existing international economic giants. For this argument to be valid, the domestic industry should be forewarned that the import protection will be cut off at some specific date. Otherwise, the infants will probably want to perpetuate their protected status. Like the proverbial son who refuses to leave home, some protected industries may resist confronting the real world indefinitely.

Finally, an argument can be made for temporary protectionist measures to prevent genuine culture shock in some developing countries. This is not so much an economic issue as it is an anthropological one that recognizes the potential for the destruction of traditional handicraft societies that a sudden, unexpected influx of machine-made goods can represent. When such an influx occurs, it frequently affects not only the economic livelihood but also the ancient cultural fabric of the community. Again, this is not an argument for permanent restrictions; it is simply an admission that it may be desirable to slow things down to give people in smaller, less-developed countries a chance to make economic adjustments.

But when the exceptions are noted and acknowledged, the fact remains that free trade is, more often than not, a worthwhile goal. Fortunately, the world's major trading partners generally recognize this fact. Since 1947, there have been significant attempts to reduce trade barriers through the **General**

Agreements for Tariffs and Trade (GATT). By the early 1980s, various tariff-negotiation milestones (the so-called "Kennedy Round" in 1967 and the "Tokyo Round" in 1979) had reduced tariffs to historically low levels. Unfortunately, the more recent "Uruguay Round" (beginning in 1986) has not been so successful—especially in the efforts to break down barriers in farm commodities, telecommunications, and financial services. The United States, it should be noted, has achieved real successes in evolving a regional free trade bloc, sometimes called the **North American Free Trade Agreement (NAFTA)** between the United States, Mexico, and Canada. NAFTA, the European Community, and a regional trade bloc emerging in Asia (headed by Japan) will be interesting to watch as we move into the twenty-first century.

In conclusion, there will always be political and economic pressures to restrict trade, even after agreements have been made; thus there's always the threat of a dangerous trade war lurking in the background. We should be on guard.

But even without a trade war, periodic imbalances of trade still pose knotty problems for any country. It's time to take a closer look at the age-old struggle of how countries balance their international payments.

Questions for Thought and Discussion

1. If trade is so good for all countries, then why shouldn't all tariffs and quotas be dropped?
2. Given a traditional economic system, what kinds of changes must be made in subsistence agrarian societies to generate the necessary surpluses for trade to take place?
3. In the 1980s, many U.S. manufacturing jobs were lost to foreign competitors and plant modernizations. What can/ should society do to assist these dislocated workers? Specify appropriate policies, costs, and benefits.
4. "Trade provides the same kinds of improvements in well-being that a country gains from having additional economic resources." Explain the reasoning behind this statement.

NEW PERSPECTIVES

Comparative Advantage . . . Mexican Style

Often a country's comparative advantage is obvious: relatively inexpensive labor in Taiwan and Hong Kong; productive farmland in North America and Argentina; for innovative and efficient manufacturing technologies, Japan and Germany come to mind.

Mexico, however, has a major export based on a rather unconventional comparative advantage. The export in question is the Mexican soap opera! And the comparative advantage? It apparently comes from the Mexican penchant toward "emotional extremes." In fact, one of the directors of a popular Mexican soap (or "telenovela" as they are called in Mexico) says that his series' success comes from the fact that in his country,

> . . . emotions and actions tend toward dramatic extremes . . . the soap opera is a reflection of reality, not a distortion of it. . . . *

And a success they are! Mexico exports adaptations of their soaps to some 59 countries around the world. In 1991, for example, a Mexican soap series was the number one program in South Korea. In Spain, it was reported that downtown merchants were forced to adjust store hours "to avoid conflict with the broadcast of a Mexican telenovela."

Just as the United States sells overseas rights to broadcast NBA basketball games or the British export Wimbledon Tennis Championships, the Mexicans too generate income and gain valuable foreign exchange through selling their programming specialty to foreign countries.

Question: Find out what your state (or city) exports abroad. Identify, if you can, the specific comparative advantage that is the basis for its successful export.

Question: Make a list of American cultural traits, both real and stereotypical (past and present) that have been portrayed in American movies and TV programming. Assuming that many of these shows are viewed by people in foreign countries, comment on how foreigners might see Americans.

---

* Moffett, Matt. "All the World Sobs Over Mexican Soaps, 3-Hankie Exports— Will Sweet Little Guadalupe Find Love with Alfredo? Stay Tuned—in Istanbul." *The Wall Street Journal*, Jan. 9, 1992: p. 1.

11

The Problems of Trade

Remember the imaginary trade between Wisconsin and Florida in the previous chapter? This example illustrates the key concept that the principles of specialization and comparative advantage apply equally to all forms of trade—between states, between regions, between countries. Then why does it seem to be more difficult to make trading arrangements in the international sphere than it does in the domestic sphere? The question leads us to one of the most interesting issues in economics—the **balance-of-payments** problem.

Let's return to our trading arrangement between Wisconsin and Florida. If Wisconsin imports more from Florida than it exports to Florida, then we say that Wisconsin is experiencing an "unfavorable balance of trade." However, neither state gets very excited about this trade imbalance. Why not? The answer is because the entire United States uses the same currency.

If Florida businesses collect a surplus of Wisconsin dollars, they can easily spend them in Florida—or, for that matter, anywhere in the United States. In contrast, if the United States experiences an unfavorable balance of trade with Japan, the Japanese will accumulate extra dollars that, generally speaking, cannot be spent in Japan. If this imbalance continues, the Japanese will be faced with the problem of what to do with all their dollars. Thus, unlike trade between individual states, trade between countries ought to *roughly balance out over time;* otherwise, the surplus country will build up quantities of foreign currency while it sacrifices real goods and services.

What mechanisms or policies are available to bring imbalanced international trade back into balance? There have, in fact, been three major approaches to dealing with this situation. One of the earliest mechanisms to help a country solve its trade imbalance was the **classical gold-flow model,** originally described by philosopher-economist David Hume in 1752. Let's start by taking a look at this interesting idea.

Classical Gold Flow

For the classical model to work, David Hume assumed that all the countries involved in trade had to be on both international and domestic gold standards.

When trading countries go on an **international gold standard,** it means that traders from a foreign country who wind up with a surplus of, say, dollars have the right to trade those dollars for U.S. gold. If, on the other hand, traders from the United States wind up with a trade surplus, they have the right to obtain foreign gold for their surplus currencies.

To be on a **domestic gold standard** means that every dollar in circulation must be backed up by an equivalent amount of gold. A country's money supply therefore depends on how much gold it has. After losing some of its gold to a foreign country, for example, the United States will be forced to reduce its domestic money supply because it now has less gold with which to back that money supply up. On the other hand, if U.S. gold holdings increase, then the U.S. money supply will automatically increase too.

Before this model can be used to solve a balance-of-payments problem, one further assumption needs to be spelled out: the linkage between money and prices through the so-called **quantity theory of money.** This theory can be summarized quite neatly as

$$MV = PQ$$

where M is the money supply, V is the **velocity of money** (the

Hi! I'm David Hume. I would like to show you how two small countries can solve an imbalance of trade when they are both on an international and a domestic gold standard.

The two islands of Chetek and Mondovi are always trading between themselves. Last year things were pretty much in balance; that is, imports roughly equalled exports.

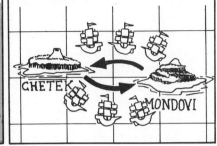

But this year Chetek imported twice as many goods from Mondovi as Mondovi imported from Chetek.

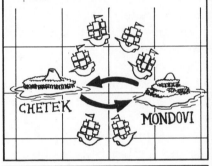

When Mondovi sells more goods, they get a surplus of Chetek currency which they trade for gold. The extra gold increases the money supply and soon pushes up Mondovi prices.

In Chetek just the opposite was happening. A loss of gold reduced their money supply and soon their prices began to go down.

High Mondovi prices therefore discourage Chetekites from buying Mondovi imports, and low Chetek prices encourage Mondovians to purchase Chetek products. Soon trade is back into balance.

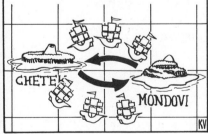

number of times an average dollar changes hands during the year), P is the general price level, and Q is the physical volume of goods and services.

Classical economists like David Hume assumed that both V and Q remain relatively constant, leaving M and P to rise or fall together. Thus, if the U.S. money supply goes up, it drives prices up, too (inflation); if M goes down, it lowers the general price level P (deflation). Keep in mind that in our simplified, classical world, all prices are assumed to be totally flexible; i.e., they can move downward or upward with equal ease.

The stage is now set for solving an imbalance problem. We'll assume that the United States suddenly finds itself in a serious trade deficit with Japan: U.S. imports to Japan are greater than U.S. exports from Japan. As a result, the Japanese receive more dollars than they can spend. Under the classical assumptions just outlined, Japanese traders exchange their surplus dollars for American gold, and the quantity of gold in the U.S. Treasury declines. This reduction in gold stock forces a reduction in the U.S. money supply, which is followed by a decrease in our prices. Falling U.S. prices, in turn, make our products less expensive and therefore more attractive to Japanese consumers. As U.S. exports expand, we find ourselves moving toward a balance-of-payments equilibrium.

While all this is going on in the United States, Japan's growing gold stock enables more money to circulate in its economy. More money (given a fixed volume of goods and services) will create Japanese inflation. Finally, high Japanese prices will discourage the Japanese from exporting goods to the United States and help to resolve the original imbalance of payments. A summary of the relevant linkages leading to this trade equilibrium are diagrammed in Figure 11-1.

Classical gold flow is a completely automatic and totally reliable system. This model operates like some self-regulating Newtonian machine, continually moving the system toward a favorable balance-of-payments equilibrium without messy maintenance or outside tinkering. So why don't we use this system today?

First, the United States is no longer on an international gold standard, nor is it on a domestic gold standard (the last vestige of gold backing disappeared in 1967). There is simply not enough gold to keep up with expanding domestic money supplies and the general growth of world trade.

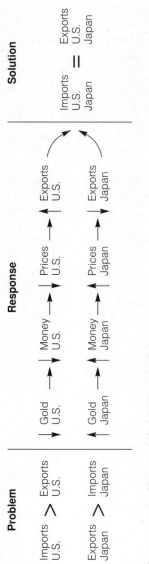

FIGURE 11-1 Classical Gold Flow model

More importantly, though, prices would probably not respond with the classical flexibility needed to make the system work even if the United States were still on the gold standard. Today, prices tend to go up and up and very rarely go down. In fact, the only time the United States has experienced general deflation in the twentieth century occurred during the Great Depression of the 1930s! If a depression is what it takes to get prices down, it's simply not worth it. There must be a better way to solve our international balance-of-payments problem. This brings us to our second method of dealing with international trade imbalances—a method that is even simpler than the classical model in many ways. It's called the **flexible exchange-rate system.**

Flexible Exchange Rates

The key to understanding flexible exchange rates is to realize that world currencies are subject to supply-and-demand markets not unlike those markets for corn or soybeans. In theory, we can draw demand-and-supply curves for every country's currency. Perhaps it would be helpful to illustrate this point by choosing one specific currency—the German mark.

We begin by asking, "Why would Americans demand German marks?" There is basically one answer: Marks are needed for American consumers to purchase German products and services. Thus, the U.S. demand for marks will reflect the demand for German imports. If American consumers suddenly want lots more German cars or cameras, they will need more marks, and the demand for marks will rise.

We then ask, "Why would the Germans want to supply us with marks?" Germany will supply the United States with marks in direct relation to its desire to purchase U.S. products and services. If Germans want a lot more American wheat or computers, for example, then the supply curve for marks will increase.

Assuming that there is an equilibrium between German and American trade, there will also be an equilibrium in the market for marks. This example is illustrated in Figure 11-2, where the price of a German mark (its **exchange rate**) is $0.25. We are assuming that at the $0.25 price trade between the United States and Germany is in balance.

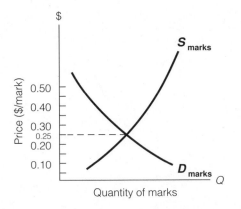

FIGURE 11-2 The supply and demand for German marks. Note that the equilibrium price of a mark is $0.25, or 25 cents.

Now let's see what happens when American consumers suddenly want a lot more German products or services or decide to travel more in Germany. They might also be interested in building U.S.-owned factories in Germany or investing in German corporate stocks. Each of these measures will contribute to a short-run U.S. balance-of-payments deficit; each of these activities will also increase the U.S. demand for German marks. We will assume that Germany is not particularly interested in purchasing any more American products, so that their willingness to supply marks remains constant. The market for marks is then altered, as demand increases in relation to a constant supply curve.

This change is shown in Figure 11-3. What is happening, of course, is that those who want additional marks *must bid up the price to get them.* This is reflected by a new equilibrium price of $0.40 (versus the old price of $0.25). As the price for marks goes up, we say the dollar is being **depreciated;** U.S. dollars are now *worth less* in relation to German marks.

In the word *depreciation,* we discover the real key to the flexible exchange-rate system. Since the dollar is now worth less, it will take more dollars to buy a given amount of German goods and services. If a bottle of German beer costs 1 mark, for example, then Americans must pay $0.40 for that bottle of beer, in contrast with the former price of $0.25 a bottle. Virtually every economic dealing with Germany will cost proportionately more: buying a Mercedes Benz, traveling to Bonn, building a

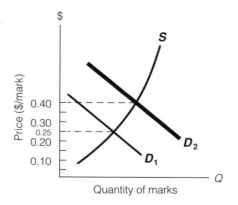

FIGURE 11-3 Assuming that U.S. citizens want to buy more German imports, to travel to Germany, or to make investments directly within the German economy, they will need (demand) more German marks than they did before. Graphically, this development will shift the demand curve to the right from D_1 to D_2. Note that this shift in demand increases the price of a mark from $0.25 to $0.40.

soap factory in Cologne, or buying a share of stock in a German company. As dollars depreciate relative to the mark, Americans will likely cut back their German purchases and travel plans, which will in turn tend to bring trade back into balance.

Note that the change in the currency's equilibrium price represents not only **depreciation** for the U.S. dollar but also **appreciation** for the German mark. Germany now sees U.S. exports as less expensive (1 mark, for example, will buy $0.40 worth of U.S. goods instead of $0.25 worth) and therefore begins to increase their purchase of American products. They may also start to set up factories in, and travel more to, the United States. All of these activities should help to restore the original trade balance.

Now assume for a moment that you are planning to travel to a foreign country. How do you find out what it will cost you to purchase the foreign currency you will need? Check the business section of many major newspapers, and you will find a table listing the value of most world currencies in relationship to the dollar. Using Table 11-1, see if you can, for example, determine how much it cost in U.S. dollars to purchase a Swiss franc on April 10, 1990.

According to the table, a Swiss franc would cost you about $0.67 ($0.6750). Also, in the column "Currency per U.S. $," note that $1 will purchase 1.48 Swiss francs. Of course, international currencies rise or fall in value according to shifts in supply and

TABLE 11-1   Abbreviated Exchange-Rate Table (Thursday, February 27, 1992)

COUNTRY	U.S. $ EQUIV.	CURRENCY PER U.S. $
Argentina (Peso)	1.03	.97
Austria (Schilling)	.0869	11.51
Britain (Pound)	1.763	.5672
Canada (Dollar)	.8485	1.1785
China (Renminbi)	.1832	5.46
France (Franc)	.1798	5.56
India (Rupee)	.0382	26.18
Ireland (Punt)	1.6310	.6131
Israel (Shekel)	.4296	2.328
Italy (Lira)	.000814	1228.06
Japan (Yen)	.00775	129.07
Mexico (Peso)	.000327	3061.01
Netherland (Guilder)	.5431	1.841
Pakistan (Rupee)	.0408	24.52
Philippines (Peso)	.0393	25.42
South Korea (Won)	.00133	753.5
Spain (Peseta)	.0097	102.64
Sweden (Krona)	.1685	5.935
Switzerland (Franc)	.6750	1.48
Taiwan (Baht)	.0403	24.8
Germany (Mark)	.6112	1.636

demand. For example, in early 1985, that same Swiss franc was worth about $0.37, which means that this particular currency has nearly doubled in dollar price between 1985 and 1992. This change implies that imported Swiss products or the cost of touring Switzerland will be noticeably more expensive in the early 1990s in contrast to their prices in the mid-1980s.

If we were to compare the U.S. dollar to an average value of other currencies as a whole, we would see a considerable flip-flop in its value since the early 1970s: first, a long drift downward (dollar depreciation) during the 1970s; then a steep climb (appreciation) of approximately 60 percent from 1980 to 1985. This trend made U.S. consumers and travelers smile but, at the same time, created headaches for American export industries because U.S. products were generally more expensive in the eyes of foreign buyers. American farmers and heavy-equipment manufacturers were among those especially hurt by the 1980–1985 increase in the value of the U.S. dollar. After 1985, however, another dollar depreciation in effect reversed the respective groups who benefit (U.S. exporters) and who pay more (U.S. consumers).

The peaks and troughs of the ever-changing exchange rates are, needless to say, difficult to predict. Sometimes the speed of a currency's ascent or descent makes many exporters and central bankers uneasy, not unlike experiencing the ups and downs of a roller-coaster ride.

Still, it is this flexible exchange-rate system—with some modifications and central-bank interventions—that is working to help realign currencies throughout the world today. Before we discuss recent policies, however, we need to take a brief look at the third method of dealing with world balance-of-payments problems: the **modified gold/fixed exchange-rate system,** which dominated the international scene for almost 30 years (1944–1971). How did this system differ from the classical gold-flow model or the flexible exchange-rate system? Let's take a look.

Modified Gold/Fixed Exchange-Rate System

The system of fixed exchange began in a specific location at a specific time. Its birthplace was Bretton Woods,* New Hampshire. The year was 1944. World War II—the war that devastated much of Europe and almost all of Japan—was coming to a close. Entire economic infrastructures (factories, roads, power plants, etc.) had literally been blown apart.

The United States, however, was stronger than ever. Its economic infrastructure remained intact; its work force was basically unharmed. It was not surprising that the major industrial countries of the world looked to the United States for postwar assistance and leadership.

U.S. assistance was offered in the form of the **Marshall Plan** and the **International Bank for Reconstruction and Development.** Both of these programs poured billions of dol-

---

* The Modified Gold/Fixed Exchange Rate System is frequently called simply "the Bretton Woods System," because of the city of its birth.

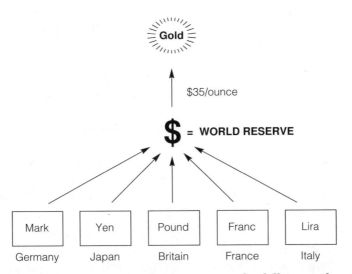

FIGURE 11-4 In the fixed exchange rate system, the dollar was the center-piece currency. The dollar, in turn, was fixed to gold at $35 per ounce.

lars into European reconstruction. In terms of international leadership, it was agreed at the 1944 Bretton Woods Conference that the world was henceforth to be on a **fixed exchange-rate system,** using the dollar as the centerpiece currency. All other major world currencies would be pegged at fixed values in relation to the dollar; the dollar, in turn, would be pegged at a fixed rate of $35 per ounce of gold. Thus, the world nations were on an international gold standard: Countries with a surplus of dollars could, if they wished, trade them for U.S. gold. However, most countries chose to keep their dollars as reserves in their international checking accounts. Dollars therefore became a kind of world legal tender. These monetary relationships are diagrammed in Figure 11-4.

Fixed exchange rates had the virtue of being resolutely stable; at the time, they were backed by gold, a strong dollar, and an unrivaled American economy. The chance, however, that a country might experience balance-of-payment difficulties still existed. Anticipating such problems, Bretton Woods officials agreed to set up an institution that could loan deficit countries the requisite amount of dollars (or other currencies) as their needs arose. The chief purpose of this **International Monetary Fund** (IMF) was to help make these short-term loans and perhaps some long-term readjustments in a country's basic exchange rate.

Suppose that some country (for example, Great Britain) kept running chronic balance-of-payments deficits. The British pound would then be overvalued in relation to other currencies and would eventually have to be devalued. How would Britain devalue the pound? British bankers would approach the IMF and request a new (lower) exchange rate for the pound in relation to the dollar; instead of $2.60 per pound, they might want to go down to, say, $2.

Devaluation may sound like a case of depreciation under a flexible exchange-rate system (discussed in the last section), but there are a couple of important differences. First, the flexible exchange-rate system adjusts automatically to short-run changes in the supply of, and demand for, a currency. In the case of the devaluation of the pound under the fixed system, the British have to *ask* the IMF for permission to adjust the exchange rate. The IMF Board of Directors thus ensures orderly readjustments in world exchange rates.

The second difference is perhaps more subtle. After devaluation, the British pound is worth less not only in relation to the U.S. dollar but also to *all other currencies* valued in relation to the dollar (see Figure 11-4). To review, *depreciation* is the reduction of the value of a currency in relation to the value of *one* other currency; *devaluation* is the reduction of the value of a currency in relation to *all* other currencies.

In general, the fixed exchange-rate system worked reasonably well, but it had one overriding flaw: an overwhelming reliance on the dollar. For example, what would happen if the United States began to experience its own chronic balance-of-payments deficits—if the dollar itself became overvalued? How would you like to be holding millions of dollars in your international checking account, believing these dollars would always be worth a certain amount in terms of other currencies (as well as gold), and then, unexpectedly have the United States devalue the dollar? This could be done by simply raising the dollar's par value with gold from $35 per ounce to some higher amount. If, for example, the United States raised the price of gold to, say, $70 per ounce, then the value of your foreign-held dollars (which you've retained because you have faith in the stability of the fixed exchange-rate system) would be cut in half! The fixed exchange-rate system had a structural inability to effectively deal with the possible devaluation of the dollar.

For a long time, however, it wasn't necessary to devalue the dollar. Postwar Europe, hungry for U.S. consumer goods and industrial products, demanded lots of U.S. dollars. However, beginning in the mid-1950s and continuing into the 1960s, problematic U.S. trade deficits occurred year after year.

One quite predictable reason for this was that the Europeans, Japanese, and other Pacific Rim countries (PRCs) eventually began to close the postwar productivity gap. Especially in Germany and Japan, the bombed-out factories and infrastructures were often replaced with the most modern facilities available. Also, the U.S. productivity growth rate fell from a relatively high 3 percent increase per year (the average rate from 1948 to 1966) down to 2 percent per year (from 1966 to 1973); for the rest of the 1970s, it averaged only about 1 percent per year. Not only did Japanese and German productivity increase more rapidly than U.S. productivity, but other energetic Asian economies, including Taiwan, South Korea, Singapore, and Hong Kong, began to expand their own export production and to make significant inroads into U.S. markets.

An additional problem—the relatively high U.S. inflation rate—worsened during the mid- and late 1960s. Higher U.S. prices discouraged foreign buyers and hurt the U.S. balance of payments. The American military presence overseas represented another net outflow of dollars. In addition, the costly Vietnam War undoubtedly contributed to U.S. inflation and trade deficits as well.

Another development that diminished U.S. exports was the formation of the **European Community,** or the **Common Market,** which promoted free trade within its borders but often set up barriers to trade with the rest of the world, including the United States. To compete effectively within Common Market countries, U.S. corporations often had to make *direct investments* within the represented countries by setting up American factories on European soil. These direct investments again contributed to a net outflow of dollars and—in the short run at least—hurt the U.S. balance of payments.

Each new problem enlarged U.S. deficits more and more. Of course, the modified gold/fixed exchange-rate system did provide some techniques (short of devaluation) for coping with this increasing deficit. First, it was possible to exchange gold for surplus dollars, as originally intended under the Bretton Woods agreement. Recall that the United States agreed to sell gold to foreign monetary authorities at the fixed rate of $35 per ounce. Indeed, countries like France and Austria often insisted on exchanging their surplus dollars for gold. Exchanging gold, however, had its drawbacks: the U.S. gold stock was not unlimited. Originally worth some $25 billion right after World War II, U.S. gold reserves had shrunk to less than 50 percent of that amount two decades later.

Members of the U.S. Congress were tempted to solve the imbalance problem by restricting foreign goods. In Chapter 10, we found that such protectionist policies are self-defeating and can easily set off a restrictive trade war. Fortunately, the protectionists didn't get very far. Legislators did pass laws that helped to a certain degree. Efforts to "tie" foreign aid (require that the recipient country purchase U.S. products) were instituted. Restrictions were also placed on the amount of imported goods that an American tourist could bring back duty free. But these and other legislative efforts did not really solve the basic problem of an overvalued dollar. Still, the United States didn't want to devalue its currency unless it was absolutely necessary.

Perhaps the easiest way to deal with the U.S. deficit was to convince foreign monetary authorities to hold onto their surplus dollars. Many countries kept dollars strictly for legal tender; others wanted interest-bearing dollar assets. If U.S. interest rates were relatively high compared to interest rates on alternative investments, then foreigners might be in no hurry to make gold exchanges.

These techniques, in addition to selling gold and arranging for assistance from the IMF, helped the United States to hang on to the Bretton Woods system through the 1960s. But by the early 1970s, foreign dollar claims were skyrocketing, the U.S. gold supply was dwindling to an all-time low, and U.S. balance-of-payments deficits continued to grow. Something had to be done to avert an international dollar crisis. The Bretton Woods fixed exchange-rate system was simply not compatible with the realities of current international trade.

The dramatic moment finally came on August 15, 1971, when President Richard Nixon suspended all gold transactions. In effect, the old system of gold convertibility went out the window. The dollar was now allowed to float; its future value was to be determined primarily by the forces of supply and demand. By 1973, the dollar had depreciated significantly compared to most of the world's major currencies. The prices of many imports—from German Volkswagons to Japanese Datsuns, from Middle Eastern oil to Swiss watches—went up accordingly. A new economic era had arrived.

Of course, the flexible exchange-rate system of the 1970s and 1980s didn't solve all U.S. balance-of-payments problems. Various governments (including the U.S. government) were not shy about intervening against speculators and other threats to their currencies, at times preventing proper currency realignments. The United States also found itself hurt by the emergence of an effective world oil cartel (OPEC) that created a sudden increase in the price of crude oil in the 1970s, contributing to a large net outflow of U.S. dollars. In the first half of the 1980s, the United States witnessed something new (and, to a large degree, unanticipated)—a phenomenal increase in the dollar's average exchange value against most major foreign currencies. Economists attribute this development to a strong foreign-dollar demand for investments in the United States. Why did this take place?

For one thing, the United States appeared to be a safe haven in a world of political uncertainty. Also, foreigners felt that the United States had good investment opportunities, especially in the years of a relatively high gross domestic product (GDP). And finally, high real-interest rates (due to ebbing U.S. inflation) made many American investments that much more attractive. Unfortunately, this increase in the dollar's international value hurt many traditional U.S. exporting industries and contributed to additional deficits in U.S. balance-of-payment merchandise accounts.

The United States as a Debtor Nation

Perhaps the most dramatic outcome of these developments was the fact that the United States officially became a net debtor nation in 1985, meaning that the value of foreign investments (stocks, bonds, government securities, real estate, bank deposits, etc.) in the United States exceeded its total investments in other countries. These foreign investments could put the United States in a potentially more vulnerable economic position, especially if this debtor status worsens progressively. Some analysts fear that such a trend might increase the possibility (perhaps the probability) of large, even violent, currency readjustments that would be beyond the nation's control. Sudden currency adjustments could, in turn, dramatically and adversely impact on inflation and even jeopardize real growth and employment.

Historian Arthur Schlesinger, Jr., for one, is concerned about what he sees as a parallel with the decline of the British Empire. In his view, the United States is suffering from the slow, but steady, erosion of its financial and, possibly, its military independence. In an editorial in *The Wall Street Journal*, Schlesinger writes:

> Consider. . . the national security implications if our creditors should register disapproval of government policies by dumping Treasury securities and other holdings on the market. . . . Never before in American history has the United States been so much at the mercy of decisions made by foreigners. As a creditor nation in the nineteenth century, Britain ruled the waves; as a debtor nation in the twentieth century, it began to sink beneath them. . . . Now we are approaching Britain's condition of economic vulnerability. . . .[42]

In the same editorial, Schlesinger quotes Robert Gilpin, political science analyst at Princeton: "It would be very difficult for the United States to fight another war on the same scale as the Korean or Vietnamese conflicts without Japanese permission and financial support of the dollar. . . . "

These comments may constitute an extreme position on America's international economic vulnerability. Other observers are not nearly as concerned. Princeton economist William J. Baumol reminds *Wall Street Journal* readers that the United States continues to have the highest absolute productivity level in the world, and he is also impressed to note that some U.S. industries, like steel, "rise from the dead"[43] with new and efficient "mini-mills." Economist Herbert Stein, with an unconventional view, goes one step further, quoting the results of recent studies that claim the United States still has a healthy lead in per-capita standard of living and ending his article, "Who's Number One? Who Cares?":

> Our real problem . . . is not to get richer than someone else or to get richer faster than someone else but to be as good as we can be, and better than we have been, in areas of our serious deficiencies, such as homelessness, poverty, ignorance, and crime.[44]

Keep in mind, too, that unlike the economies of some European and Asian countries, the U.S. economy is not quite as dependent on its foreign-trade sector because the United States produces 85 to 90 percent of its domestically consumed goods and services within its own borders. Even in the vulnerable area of petroleum, the United States demonstrated a surprising adaptability to the conservation of oil and the development of alternative energy strategies under the heat of rapidly rising oil prices during the 1970s. At that time, you could hardly pick up a popular magazine without seeing articles on energy conservation, superinsulation, earth-sheltered homes, fuel-efficient cars, and the like.

Also, the United States is still generally competitive in many of its traditional export industries, including chemicals, hotels and restaurants, soft drinks, paper products, aircraft, telecommunications, food and fiber, insurance, office machines, banking, farm machinery, computers, TV sit-coms, and sports programming, just to name a few. Finally, we should recognize that even though the U.S. productivity growth rate has slowed significantly, the American output per worker hour (in absolute terms) is still higher than it is in most other industrialized countries.

In summary, the United States will continue to face various international trade problems in the future and, if certain trends (such as deficits and low productivity growth) become chronic problems, will be courting economic trouble in future decades. Yet in relation to the majority of the world's people, who live in the less-developed Third World countries, Americans are still very well off indeed. Perhaps now it is time to leave U.S. shores behind and journey to these struggling nations. What is life like in the developing countries? More importantly, what does the future hold for them?

QUESTIONS FOR THOUGHT AND DISCUSSION

1. Why don't all countries adopt the same currency in order to solve the balance-of-payments problem?
2. What would happen if all countries devalued their currencies by the same percentage?

3. How would Hume's Gold Flow model be affected if the velocity of money V and the physical volume of goods and services Q were not held constant?

4. During the mid-1980s, spokespersons for U.S. export industries argued that high U.S. interest rates were partially responsible for their weakened competitive positions in world markets. Explain how this might be possible.

5. Would it be a good idea to return to the international gold standard? Why or why not?

NEW PERSPECTIVES

Japanese Trade and Investments . . . Another Pearl Harbor?

Poets know it. So do dictators and industry propagandists. What they know well is *the power of symbolic metaphor!* For example, when Lee Iacocca returned from Japan in early 1992,* he made a reference to Pearl Harbor in an appearance before the Economic Club of Detroit. The metaphoric implications? Apparently the United States was once again a victim of a "sneak attack"—not bombers this time, but an invasion of goods and services as well as Japanese-owned factories located in the heartland of America.

It is a fact that the United States has run chronic trade deficits with Japan. And too, Japan's "surplus" dollars often return to our shores in the form of direct investments (i.e., U.S.-based factories), as well as purchases of commercial real estate. But is the Pearl Harbor imagery really appropriate? And perhaps even more important, is it helpful in our search for solutions to our trade problems?

Harvard economist Robert Reich doesn't think so. In his essay "Remembering Pearl Harbor—Too Often,"** Reich says that this metaphor is not only misleading, but its frequent use by politicians and industrialists is truly counterproductive to our interests. To the implication that the U.S. is being attacked, Reich says,

> The metaphor of a Japanese 'attack' began to be used in the early 1970s to describe Japan's increasing shares of the American steel, textile, and television markets. British, Dutch, and West German imports had already gained substantial shares of several markets such as automobiles and beer, but their successes were never described as 'attacks.'

* Iacocca was a member of a group of American industrialists accompanying President Bush to Japan.
** Reich, Robert B. "Remembering Pearl Harbor—Too Often." *Harpers,* Jan., 1992: pp. 20–21.

What about the notion that Japan, having lost World War II, was now successfully returning to "raid" American industries and markets? Once more, Reich wonders why Japan is singled out:

> Here again, there was nothing unusual about foreign direct investments in the United States. The British own twice as much of America as do the Japanese—including American icons like Burger King—and yet we never speak of the British 'raiding' America.

Reich goes on to actually praise Japanese managers (especially in the auto industry) for their success in running profitable U.S.-based operations while at the same time, giving American workers "more training, better wages, and more job security than Iacocca ever dreamed of giving his own employees."

Question: Why are the Japanese singled out with emotion-packed metaphors, when investors in other nations are making similar investments and buy-outs in the U.S.? And too, why is the consumer's point of view so rarely mentioned in the debate? (How would you represent the consumer's viewpoint?)

Question: What should the United States do in response to its chronic deficits with Japan? Suggest a healthy course of action for both business leaders and government policy makers.

12

World Development

In the summer of 1974, well-fed Americans didn't seem quite so hostile to high food prices as they had been the previous year. One explanation might have been the depressing stories in major newsmagazines and on television—not stories of high food prices but stories of no food at all. During that summer, there was very little food for millions of North Africans as they suffered through their sixth straight year of drought. A half million men, women, and children were already dead, and an estimated 10 million more were living at near-starvation levels throughout the North African famine belt.

Rain did finally arrive, but these horrifying statistics were repeated with grim cyclic regularity in the mid-1980s and again in early 1990, exposing the developed world to its first close-up coverage of the frightening realities of mass starvation. The world could no longer ignore the suffering: The catastrophe was simply too large.

Of course, these crises would pass, as many others had for centuries before them. Yet the uneasy feeling around the world could not be forgotten as national leaders discussed the possibility that famine might eventually affect not just millions, but billions of people in low-income countries.

There is no doubt that the industrialized countries will have enough food for years to come. Even under the worst economic conditions, most people in the "over-developed" nations will continue to eat luxuriously[45] and even to feed protein-rich food to their pets. They have the income and can generate effective demand.

But what about the approximately 3 billion people in the less-developed Third World countries? What are their chances for widespread economic development? The problem of mass poverty must be considered one of the major global issues of our time.

Regions under consideration include most of Asia (except Japan, South Korea, and Taiwan), most of black Africa, and Latin America. Although some of these countries are monetarily better off than others, we are essentially talking about roughly three-fifths of the world's current population. Let's take a moment to examine some of the general characteristics common to many of these poorer countries.

Education and Nutrition

Certainly one common element in most low-income countries is the problem of mass illiteracy. Scarce resources often go toward the education of elite classes, who are taught an outmoded, colonial curriculum in schools that deemphasize the skills needed for economic development. For prestigious reasons, students often choose "literate" professions or civil-service training instead of business, farming, trades, or engineering. These new workers move into a world of bureaucratic desks and white shirts, rather than one of farms and factories.

Other students come to the United States, England, or France to receive legal or other professional training to eventually serve an upper-class clientele. Some never return to their homelands. Not only does this kind of investment use of scarce public money not fund adult literacy classes and basic mechanical, agricultural, and paramedic training, but it also tends to reinforce class consciousness and widen income differentials.

Nutrition is also often a problem. Even without famine conditions, poor countries have always had difficulty obtaining food with adequate protein. Protein deficiency, in turn, may

eventually result in the crippling disease known as *kwashiorkor.*
The victims, almost always children, are seen in photographs
with large, protruding bellies and thin, reddish hair. Another
nutritional disease, *xerophthalmia,* the result of a deficiency in
vitamin A, exposes millions of people to a bacterial eye infection
that can lead to permanent blindness. Many other diseases
resulting from nutritional deficiencies impair mental and physical performance in one way or another.

Do these nutritional problems mean that industrialized
countries ought to supply poorer countries with free food? This
generosity would, ironically, probably do more harm than good
(at least in the long run) since it would very likely obstruct the
evolution of free market agricultural industries in less-developed
nations as well as in former communist countries like Russia or
Czechoslovakia. To illustrate this point, imagine the impact of
some "benevolent" country giving free milk to everyone in the
United States. In a short period of time, much of the U.S. dairy
industry would be forced into bankruptcy, and American consumers would eventually be dependent on the charity of this
benefactor.

What the Third World farmer needs is really no different from what other successful farmers require to be productive: positive economic incentives, such as reasonably high, stable commodity prices, access to land, credit, marketing cooperatives, and appropriate farm technology.[46] Frequently, a successful agricultural industry can get under way by simply eliminating obstacles that already exist, including elitist land-tenure arrangements and artificially low prices imposed by the government to placate urban workers. Indeed, a successful agrarian base is often the best method of providing food to the masses and upgrading nutritional levels.

Capital and Productivity

In general, Third World countries lack productive capital, including laborsaving tools and machines. Indeed, the average African or Asian peasant does use a certain amount of low-level capital goods—hoes, wooden plows, manual systems for irrigation, and so forth—but some capital is extremely unproductive.

The key word here is *productivity.* The growth process in capital-intensive countries goes something like this. First, highly productive labor generates a large amount of output, which translates into relatively high incomes for workers. High wage rates increase production costs, forcing producers to develop ever new productive technologies. Increased technologies in turn increase productivity, and the growth sequence begins all over again.

On the other hand, less-developed countries cannot generate high incomes because their capital resources generate extremely low productivity. The result is a vicious circle of poverty and underdevelopment in the form of low productivity, low incomes, and low consumption levels. The overall productivity level in most poor countries is so low that a large percentage of the people live at the subsistence level, producing so little that they are forced to exist not much above the *survival line.*

Living near the margin of survival with little hope of upward mobility distinguishes the poor of the Third World countries from the poor of the industrialized countries:

> Living poor is like being sentenced to exist in a stormy sea in a battered canoe, requiring all your strength simply to keep afloat; there is never any question of reaching a destination. True poverty is a state of perpetual crisis, and one wave just a little bigger

or coming from an unexpected direction can and usually does wreck things. Some benevolent ignorance denies a poor man the ability to see the squalid sequence of his life, except very rarely; he views it rather as a disconnected string of unfortunate sadness. Never having paddled on a calm sea, he is unable to imagine one. I think if he could connect the chronic hunger, the sickness, the death of his children, the almost unrelieved physical and emotional tension into the pattern that his life inevitably takes, he would kill himself.[47]

Thus, the poor in the developing countries live with uncertainty under substandard conditions. Illiteracy, poor physical and mental health, and hunger are combined with a traditional economic system based on unskilled labor and low-productivity tools.

Institutional Barriers

One much less visible element of underdevelopment may be even more harmful to developmental efforts than a lack of productive resources. Economists call this area **institutional barriers to change.** It includes adverse power relationships, elitist political systems, cultural traditions, tribalism, graft and corruption, and the impact of foreign values. Relevant questions pertaining to institutional problems might include:

- How do traditional cultural practices affect developmental efforts?
- How equal or unequal is the distribution of wealth and income?
- What percentage of agricultural workers own no land?
- What role do foreign values and economic interests play in Third World development?
- How strong is national cohesiveness? How do the loyalties of citizens to the nation state (to its laws, taxes, language, etc.) compare to tribal or traditional religious loyalties?

Population

Let's begin with the question of traditional culture and its effect on economic development. Many economists feel that the major obstacle to economic betterment is the simple desire to have a large family. Among low-income, traditional communities, we find a high degree of social status (as well as future "social security") given to parents who have many surviving children. Yet such a simple cultural value can create social and economic problems. A growth rate of 2 percent, for example, can double a population in about 35 years. Although some Third World countries exceed this 2 percent figure, the average growth rate for the world as a whole is about 1.7 percent. Still, there will probably be more than 6 billion people in our world by the year 2000—1 billion more than today's figure.

These numbers are perhaps more meaningful when put into historical perspective. For example, it took about 2 million years for the human species to bring the world population up to its first billion people. The second billion were added in about 100 years; the third billion, in just 30 years; the fourth, in only 15. The fifth billion was added within fairly recent history— from 1974 to 1987, or in roughly thirteen years! If the 1.7 percent population growth rate figure holds, approximately 8 billion people will be living in this world by the year 2015, and 16 billion will be living here only one generation later (by the year 2055). Most of these increases will be in the populations of less-developed countries.

These figures are staggering indeed. Such large numbers will probably be modified, either by rising overall death rates (due to possible starvation, military conflicts, epidemics, general stress) or, more humanely, declining overall birth rates. Indeed, population experts have pointed out that much more can still be done in the area of birth control and family planning. It is interesting to note that the countries that are currently most successful at controlling their growth rates are either authoritarian (mainland China, for example) or have demonstrated rapid economic growth at some time (as Taiwan, Singapore, and Hong Kong have). Ironically, the best and least-repressive method of reversing attitudes about family size is through the process of community development: helping children to survive by offering them better health care and equally important, by providing women with alternatives to childbearing in the form of outside work opportunities. Indeed, after years of traveling, researching, and evaluating family-planning programs, writer Pranay Gupta, in his book *The Crowded Earth,* put the greatest emphasis on the importance of upgrading the economic status of women:

> I found during my travels that more and more women also seem to want to get out of their homes to involve themselves in economic activities, a situation that could eventually lead to even more women producing fewer children and thus bring down Asian nations' annual population growth rates. The experience of places such as Bali, Sri Lanka, South Korea, and the southern Indian state of Kerela has shown that, where women were brought into the economic mainstream through increased female education and employment, there was not only an overall decline in the population growth rate but also an improvement in the content and pace of development and in the general quality of life of the entire community.[48]

Yet for many of the poorest Third World countries, economic opportunities, health-care resources, and other fruits of economic development are often beyond the reach of individuals, families, and communities caught in the vicious circle of poverty. On the one hand, high population growth rates stifle the potential for economic development; on the other hand, women want fewer children only when they have access to greater opportunities and are assured that their children have a high probability of survival. Can anything be done about this dilemma?

Perhaps one answer is economic assistance from the developed countries, but it should not be the typical kind of aid that finances such impressive, capital-intensive projects as dams, army installations, airports, and luxury hotels. Instead, it should be in the form of financial and technical assistance to promote local projects that offer widespread benefits in nutrition, health, education, clean water, housing, small-scale rural technologies, and where requested, assistance in family-planning projects. It's doubtful that these people-oriented investments will increase the Gross Domestic Product as much as a new steel mill or a hydroelectric plant would, but a more equal distribution of income and the possible reduction of population rates may prove to be far more beneficial in the long run.

Wealth and Income Distribution

Another major obstacle to Third World development is the uneven concentration of power, wealth, and income. To understand the distribution of wealth and power in underdeveloped countries, we must first grasp the importance of land ownership. Poor countries are often agrarian societies in which more than 75 percent of the population works and lives in rural areas (compared to 5 percent of the population of the United States, for example.

In such communities, prestige, wealth, and power are measured not so much by capital, money, or material goods but by the amount of land a person controls. Think, for example, of the Philippines—a country that has shown some economic growth but little widespread development—where well over 50 percent of all agricultural workers are landless. Or we could journey to Latin America, where magnificent estates, each tens of thousands of acres, are owned by only a few families. We could also find many great plantations extending for miles throughout the fertile regions of Africa and Asia.

These vast acreages and plantations produce tremendous riches for their owners but usually continued poverty and dependence for the people who work or rent the land:

> In South America, the poor man is an ignorant man, unaware of the forces that shape his destiny. The shattering truth—that he is kept poor and ignorant as the principal and unspoken component of national policy—escapes him. He cries for land reform, a system of farm loans that will carry him along between crops, unaware that the national economy in almost every country sustained by a one-crop export commodity depends for its success on an unlimited supply of cheap labor. Ecuador needs poor men to compete in the world banana market; Brazil needs poverty to sell its coffee; and so on.[49]

Concentrated wealth, however, is not limited to local landlords and the traditional elite classes. Some foreigners, including former colonists who continue to live in underdeveloped countries, own immense parcels of property. Also, foreign interests frequently dominate the mining sectors that extract large amounts of raw materials from beneath the earth's surface: tin from Bolivia, petroleum from Nigeria and Mexico, tropical hardwoods from Central America, copper from Zambia and Chile, aluminum ore from Jamaica and Guinea. The list of foreign investments is extensive. Although they may bring some economic advantages to local workers, the long-run benefits to the poor of such investments are questionable in view of the exported profits, the all too frequent environmental damage caused by such operations as deforestation and open-pit mining, the continued dependence on foreign business, the strain created by unequal growth, and the tremendous reliance on a minimal number of exports to earn foreign exchange.

This last point takes on even greater significance when we learn that about 50 percent of the foreign exchange for a sizable group of developing countries is earned by the export of only one or two raw materials. For example, this means that Bolivia's ability to purchase imports (capital goods, food, consumer products, and so on) is largely dependent on how much foreign exchange the country can earn from exporting tin. Under these conditions, a small drop in tin prices could bring tremendous financial problems to Bolivia. Its foreign exchange earnings would drop significantly, its consumption of imports would be curtailed, its balance of payments would take a turn for the worse, and its major developmental projects might have to be cut back—all because of a relatively small drop in the price of tin.

Manufacturing industries are frequently dominated by foreign interests, too. Indeed, our journey to typical Third World countries would not be complete without a visit to the industrial parks on the fringes of major capital cities, where Westerners would feel quite at home in the presence of such familiar corporations as Coca-Cola, Ford, Union Carbide, and Texaco, not to mention branch factories of British, Japanese, German, French, and Dutch firms. These **multinational corporations** manufacture everything from soaps, shoes, and ballpoint pens to bicycles and portable radios. Domestic manufacturing, in turn, may be stifled because small-scale local operations usually cannot compete with these giant foreign companies.

The lopsided distribution of wealth and the dominance of foreign interests in the Third World countries can erode the incentive for local economic development. Why build up a rural homestead if you don't own the land and can't benefit from your labors? Why attempt to compete with giant corporations when you are at a disadvantage in all phases of operation, from obtaining raw materials to marketing the product?

What can be done about institutional problems in underdeveloped nations? Some economists believe that, over time, powerful governments can force the necessary reforms and remove the obstacles to economic betterment. The centralized authorities must have the means and the will to radically alter land-tenure relationships, to reduce the enormous economic and social inequalities, and to evolve an effective program of population control combined with mass health and hygienic improvements.

Governments must also facilitate the emergence of local entrepreneurs and create economic environments, particularly around cities, that are conducive to the critical process of import replacement.[50] They must encourage national savings, so that financial capital is available for business loans and essential public services. Equally importantly, they need to safeguard traditional communities that want to achieve economic self-reliance in their own ways. Governments must learn to recognize when it is better to keep out of economic affairs and when it is correct to step in.

Indeed, these are difficult tasks for these nations. Many poor countries presently lack the sense of national legitimacy, unity, and long-term stability needed to institute such far-reaching economic and social changes. Some governments will continue to be corrupt and unresponsive to national economic needs. Others will promote economic and political democracy and try to find the right balance between government intervention and the encouragement of independent action and private incentives.

Thus, one of the major problems in economics today is how highly developed countries can help bring about the changes necessary to increase the economic well-being of less-developed countries. A sharing of resources and know-how and a willingness to make some sacrifices will help to reduce the world's gross economic imbalances.

However, if economic equality is achieved in terms of successful development—especially if that development replicates Western industrial growth—then a new irony will arise, an irony that is both disturbing and, from a political viewpoint, perplexing. That subject, our final topic in this book, is the relationship between world development and global pollution.

World Development and Global Pollution

The air you breathe may seem clean to you. Of course in some notorious metropolitan areas, such as Los Angeles; Mexico City; Lagos, Nigeria; and Krakow, Poland, there is more often than not, a disagreeable smog which we know causes respiratory and

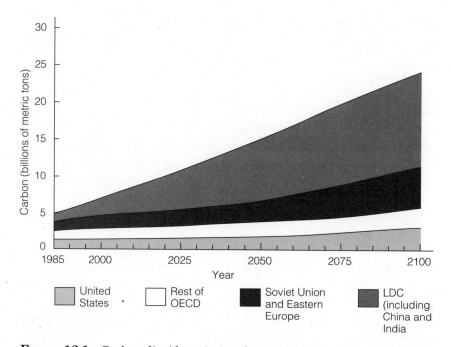

FIGURE 12-1 Carbon-dioxide emissions by region. The less-developed countries' (LDC's) share of CO_2 emissions is projected to grow rapidly; the relative U.S. share is projected to decline. (Source: President's Economic Report: 1991)

other well-documented health problems. But even in small towns and villages, you will find air pollutants derived from a variety of sources. In one test of air quality, biologists look for the presence or absence of lichens—the lovely, colorful, scale-like growths that cling to rocks and trees in noncity environments. But the sensitivity of lichens to even low levels of air pollution makes them a rare sight in populated areas. Even more subtle, invisible air contaminants are, unfortunately, becoming more and more prevalent no matter where on earth measurements are made.

Traces of synthetic chemicals plus carbon and sulfur dioxide (both byproducts of fossil-fuel combustion) are intermixing throughout the global atmosphere. These emissions are mainly the result of human activities connected with industrialization and economic development. Indeed, the President's *Economic Report to Congress* (1990) expresses great concern about the levels of current and projected future emissions; its conclusion makes no pretense that the solution to reducing these gases will be a simple one. In one chart (Figure 12-1), the report indicates that the greatest increases in carbon dioxide (CO_2) between the years 2000 and 2100 will be in Third World countries.

For example, consider China—a country that currently has the largest coal reserves in the world and plans to double its coal consumption by the end of the 1990s.

Yet, even without any additional CO_2 releases, we know that since the Industrial Revolution, economic activity has already increased the concentration of this gas by roughly 25 percent (from 280 parts per million* to approximately 360 ppm). The result is the very real possibility of global warming or the so-called *greenhouse effect.* Setting aside for a moment the honest differences of climatologists as to whether warming has already begun, author Bill McKibben, in his book *The End of Nature,* asks us to pause and reflect on the fact that we have already altered the earth's atmosphere:

> Most discussions of the greenhouse gases rush immediately to their future consequences—is the sea going to rise?—without pausing to let the simple fact of what has already happened sink in. The air around us, even where it is clean, and smells like spring, and is filled with birds, is *different,* significantly changed.[51]

Global warming, according to theorists, begins with an increase in carbon dioxide and other greenhouse gases, such as methane, chlorofluorocarbons (CFCs), and nitrous oxide. The altered atmosphere then traps additional heat, which in time increases oceanic evaporation and, hence, atmospheric water vapor. Water vapor, in turn, is an efficient greenhouse gas itself and invites further warming in a looping feedback process that may be difficult to reverse. Possible increases in average temperature range between a conservative 2 °F and a relatively large 8 °F. Temperatures in the higher range would probably be great enough to begin to melt the polar ice caps. Along with such projections, some scientists argue that the earth may have some positive, self-regulative abilities, such as the absorption of excessive CO_2 by the oceans or the possible formation of protective cumulus-type cloud covers.

---

*Preindustrial levels of CO_2 have been measured in polar ice-core samples, which contain pockets of air trapped from earlier eras.

Thus, like a football player subjected to continual bumping, bending, and bruising, the earth is also under stresses initiated by human activities and technologies and fueled by economic development. What we don't know is whether the earth's body can absorb these physical insults and—like a young, well-conditioned athlete—demonstrate a surprising resiliency, bouncing back without injury when the stress lets up.

Or is our planet more like a middle-aged, weekend player, whose nasty bruise to the knee or shoulder may be more or less permanently disabling? Environmental pessimists, looking at the ominous trends of future pollution, might remind us that even the most resilient athlete who experiences repeated traumas can be permanently injured and face severely diminished health and life processes. The precise metaphor is currently unclear, but its configuration in relation to climatic change will probably come into focus within the next 10 to 50 years.

Other concerns related to developmental activity include the ongoing destruction of tropical rain forests. When a tract of forest is cut and burned to accommodate cattle ranches or small farms or to harvest tropical woods, it compounds the greenhouse effect by reducing plant photosynthesis, which absorbs CO_2, and by releasing additional CO_2 into the atmosphere when wood is burned. It is estimated that rain-forest destruction contributes roughly 20 percent of the CO_2 buildup that climatologists have been measuring in recent decades.

Another concern related to the destruction of tropical rain forests is the extinction of entire animal and plant species. In addition to their intrinsic ecological value, the disappearance of biological diversity also has serious economic and potential health implications for human beings:

> The fact that many medicines contain active ingredients obtained from substances in plants and animals, especially those in the tropics, suggests that a reduction in diversity could represent a significant economic loss.[52]

Peter Raven, Director of the Missouri Botanical Garden, estimates that approximately one fifth of all plant and animal organisms are at risk of becoming extinct during the next 30 years.[53]

A further complication of rain-forest loss combined with climatic change is the possibility of extreme weather events. Indeed, James Lovelock, originator of the **Gaia theory** (which regards the planet as a self-regulating system that behaves as if it were a living organism) feels that the increased frequency of violent weather—superhurricanes, tornadoes, tidal waves, and record high and low temperatures—ought to be one of our main concerns:

> The destruction of the tropical rain forests and the greenhouse effect are so serious—they're not just the doom stories of scientists. . . . They will come in the form of surprises: storms of vastly greater severity than anything we've ever experienced before.[54]

Ozone depletion and acid rain are further destructive side effects of worldwide atmospheric pollution. In these areas, however, there may be greater possibilities for clean-up through the use of alternative technologies for coal-fired burning (the major cause of acid rain) or substitutes for known ozone-damaging chemicals (such as chlorofluorocarbons).

In summation, world development has produced—and probably will continue to produce—problematic environmental side effects, the most serious of which could have an adverse impact on the earth's climatic balance. Economists point out that additional research is needed and that the costs (especially before all the relevant data is in) may simply be too high, given the uncertainties. Consider, for example, all the individual workers and industry-energy related businesses (including coal mining, electric utilities, automobile manufacturers, ore and metal companies, and airlines, to name a few) that would be adversely affected by a sudden or even a slow shift away from oil and coal usage.

Other economists say that we had better not wait: If we err, we should, as the saying goes, "Err on the side of caution." Rushworth M. Kidder addresses this issue in his essay "Let's Not Wait for 'Proof' on Warning of Global Warming," when he argues that we should not evaluate clean-up costs based on certainties; instead, we should view them as costs or premiums paid on a global health-insurance policy:

> We need to change our metaphor. We need to stop looking at environmental issues as though they were court cases. We need, instead, to think of ourselves as homeowners buying insurance. You don't insure against the absolutely predictable. You protect against the possible. . . . You defend yourself against large and irreversible damages.[55]

In fact, some progress has already been made within the developed countries. The United States has initiated a reforestation plan, and some electric utilities have committed company resources to planting trees.[56] In addition, Sweden has taken the important first step of leavying a CO_2-emissions tax. Also, in the **Montreal Protocol**—a 24-nation treaty signed in 1987—the representative countries pledged to reduce ozone-depleting CFC emissions by 50 percent by the year 2000. Although the directive was strengthened in 1990, new evidence of ozone thinning, and even possible ozone "holes" over North America, accelerated the schedule of CFC production phase-out to 1995 or before. Indeed, many environmental groups see the Montreal Protocol as a model for future negotiations that will address even more complex environmental problems, such as atmospheric warming, on an international scale.[57]

Economists are beginning to rethink developmental strategies for the Third World countries that are compatible both with planetary health and with the betterment of living standards for the world's poorest nations. Working out such short- and long-term policies will be the great challenge of the coming decade and the early part of the next century. Given the complexity of these issues, economists would be well served not only to have a grounding in politics (the traditional science of *political economy*) but also to synthesize their discipline with ecology as well. Indeed, the words *economics* and *ecology* have the same root (*eco*-household), implying a knowledge of, and a concern for, the human household and nature's household. We now know that these households are interdependent and intimately linked.

For government officials, this same approach is equally valuable. Considering the enormous implications of today's decisions for tomorrow's generation and the next—in both the developed and the developing worlds—our leaders might well heed the advice of Lao Tzu, written in the fourth century B.C. Toward the end of his little book, *The Way of Life,* dedicated in part to helping the ruling class of his era, Lao Tzu writes:

> Solve the small problem before it becomes big.
> The most involved fact in the world
> Could have been faced when it was simple
> The biggest problem in the world
> Could have been solved when it was small.[58]

When we consider human impact, world economics, global population, and the environment, such advice is as solid, wise, and true today as ever.

QUESTIONS FOR THOUGHT AND DISCUSSION

1. Should all countries be developed in the pattern of industrialized Western societies?

2. In what ways is an Indian reservation in the American West like a less-developed country?

3. Consider for a moment how you did your laundry last week (i.e., did you use hot water or cold water; did you dry by the sun or by machine; did you use a phosphate or a non-phosphate detergent, etc.). How does the way you did your laundry relate to the regional, national, and global environments? Be specific.

NEW PERSPECTIVES

The Third World Poor . . . Can We "Walk in Their Shoes"?

How difficult would it be for affluent Americans to empathize with those who live in the Third World? According to the Population Reference Bureau, the United States had a 1988 per-capita GNP of $19,780 compared with the world average of $3,470.* This comparison would suggest that Americans enjoy more than five times the material standard of living of the average person living in both developed and underdeveloped countries. Compared to just the less-developed countries (whose per-capita GNP was $710), U.S. citizens had about 28 times that of an average LDC citizen. Given these statistics, is there any way that Americans can "walk in the shoes" of a typical Third World man, woman, or child?

Perhaps they can. The relief organization Oxfam America, for example, organizes an annual Hunger Banquet. When you buy a ticket, you agree to put yourself into what might be called a global lottery. According to Oxfam organizer Michael Briggs, on banquet day you'll be sitting down to eat with others in one of the three groups:

> Sixty percent sit on straw mats and eat rice and water. Twenty-five percent get a simple meal, something like rice and beans. The remaining 15 percent get a gourmet meal.**

*1990 World Population Data Sheet. Population Reference Bureau, Inc., Washington, D.C.
** Hodges, Sam. "'Walk in My Shoes' with Empathy Exercises." *The Arizona Republic*, Jan. 8, 1992: p. C2.

(continued)

Briggs commented that these percentages "reflect the distribution of world income among the haves and have-nots." Oxfam's Hunger Banquet obviously goes beyond numbers and comparative statistics: It's an experience to be felt and remembered! According to Briggs,

> To be in a room with 200 people and realize that only 15 percent are enjoying the gourmet meal and the vast majority have only rice and water is something that gets people thinking about why food is distributed so unequally.

Question: Can you devise your own activity to simulate relative deprivation? Your class might break up in small groups to brainstorm alternative ideas. If possible, choose one of the methods and try it.

Question: In light of the Population Reference Bureau's information (above), why do so many people in the developed world still feel frustration (and sometimes a sense of inadequacy) with their economic situation?

Notes

1. See, for example Bernd Heinrich's book *Bumblebee Economics* (Cambridge: Harvard, 1979), where the author examines the bumblebee's economic problem primarily in terms of energy efficiency. Another related book is Donald Worster's *Nature's Economy* (Anchor, 1979), and his title derived from the early naturalist's concept of what is today called *ecology*. Note the word *ecology* has the same root as the word *economics: oikos* (Greek for household). Thus the natural world also has cooperation, competition, inputs and outputs, maximization, etc., as nature attempts to maintain its household. Its management is not a matter of consciously choosing alternatives (as we do) but is primarily genetic, adaptive, and evolutionary. Incidently, Darwin's great insight of natural selection came to him while reading the great eighteenth-century economists, including Adam Smith and even more importantly, Thomas Malthus, whose essay *On Population* led Darwin to the idea of nature's "struggle for existence." (See *Charles Darwin's Autobiography,* New York: Henry Schuman, 1950, p. 54.)

2. See Vernon Carter and Tom Dale, *Topsoil and Civilization,* (Norman, OK: University of Oklahoma Press, 1974). This is perhaps the best reference I have seen that puts the depletion of the world's topsoil in a historical context.

3. Adam Smith, *The Wealth of Nations* (New York: Modern Library, Inc., 1977), p. 423.

4. Henry David Thoreau, *Walden* (New York: Bramhall House, 1951), pp. 29–30.

5. North Country Anvil, #4 (Box 37, Millville, MN 55957).

6. George B. Leonard, "Winning Isn't Everything, It's Nothing," *Intellectual Digest* (1973): 47.

7. Milton Friedman, "The Voucher Idea," *New York Times Magazine* (1973): 23. See also John Coons and Stephen Sugerman, *Educations by Choice: The Case for Family Control* (Berkeley, CA: University of California Press, 1978). In a modification of the public school voucher idea, Harvard economist Lester Thurow has proposed a "skill voucher" for those who do not choose to go to college. Thurow suggests such a voucher would be worth $12,000 or an amount equal to the average subsidy currently received by college students. (See *The Zero Sum Solution,* New York: Simon & Schuster, 1985, p. 205.)

8. Hugh Drummond, M.D., "Growing Old Absurd," *Mother Jones* (May, 1980).

9. For an appraisal of the financial success (or failure) of the largest mergers and LBO acquisition of the 1980s, see *Business Week* (Jan. 15, 1990).

10. Maurice Zietlin, ed., *American Society, Inc.,* (Chicago: Markham Publishing Co., 1970), pp. 513–514.

11. From *The Retreat from Riches* by Peter Passell and Leonard Ross, (New York: Viking Press, 1971), p. 36.

12. George F. Will, "Unpadding the 'Padded Society,'" *Newsweek* (1981): 100.

13. The attempts to increase productivity in some professions—high-speed drills for dentists, clinics for doctors, TV courses for educators—have undoubtedly kept costs and prices from rising higher than they would have without the productivity gain.

14. See Milton Friedman, *Capitalism and Freedom* (Chicago: University of Chicago Press, 1962), p. 150. In his chapter "Occupational Licensure" Friedman suggests that all professional licensing (including medical licensing) should be abolished in favor of a more free entry into the occupations. According to Friedman, this would ultimately lower the cost of professional services for the consumer.

15. Arthur Schlesinger, Jr., "Neo-Conservatism and the Class Struggle," *Wall Street Journal* (1981), editorial page.

16. Saul Pett, "The Bloated Bureaucracy," *St. Paul Pioneer Press* (June 4, 1981), p. 4.

17. See *The Eight Myths of Poverty* by William O'Hare. *American Demographics* (May 1986), p. 24.

18. This data was taken from Greg Duncan's book, *Years of Poverty, Years of Plenty* (Ann Arbor: Institute for Social Research, 1984).

19. Op. cit. (O'Hare), p. 25.

20. Michael Harrington, *The Other America* (New York: Macmillan, 1962), p. 13.

21. See Michael Harrington's more recent book, *The New American Poverty* (New York: Holt, Rinehart & Winston, 1984), p. 690.

22. Op. cit. (Thoreau), p. 89.

23. See footnote 7.

24. All statistics in the paragraph came from David Wessel's "Money Talks," *The Wall Street Journal* (April 8, 1992), p. A4. His source was the *Congressional Budget Office*.

25. Leopold Kohr, *Overdeveloped Nations* (New York: Schocken Books, 1978), p. 39.

26. Wade Green and Soma Golden, "Luddites Were Not all Wrong," *New York Times Magazine*. The most extreme position I have seen concerning economic growth and man's ecological destructiveness is in the poetry by the late California poet Robinson Jeffers. Many readers have interpreted his poetry to essentially say that "the human race is, in fact, not needed." See Gilbert Highet, *The Powers of Poetry* (New York: Oxford University Press, 1960), pp. 133–134.

27. Irving Kristol, "The Worst Is Yet to Come," *Wall Street Journal* (Nov. 26, 1979), p. 24.

28. Mel Ellis, "The Good Earth," *Milwaukee Journal* (1974).

29. E. B. White, *The Points of My Compass* (New York: Harper and Row, 1962), p. 67.

30. Henry Caudill, *My Land Is Dying* (New York: Dutton, 1971), p. 104.

31. James A. Michener, *The Quality of Life* (Lippincott, 1970), pp. 86–87.

32. Theodore H. White, *The Making of the President, 1964* Theodore H. White (New York: Atheneum, 1965), p. 322.

33. The highly respected forecasting newsletter, *Blue Chip Economic Indicators* (which uses a "consensus" approach of averaging the projections from approximately 50 economists) projected in March 1982 an inflation rate of 6.9% for '83, 6.6% for 1984, and 6.4% for 1985. In contrast, the actual rate (GNP Price Deflator) was 3.8% in 1983, 4.1% in 1984, and only 3.3% in 1985. (Sources: *Blue Chip Economic Indicators,* Sedona, AZ, March 10, 1982, p. 7, and *The Economic Report of the President,* Washington, D.C., Feb. 1986, p. 257.)

34. Caroline Bird, *The Invisible Scar* (New York: David McKay, 1966), pp. 26, 27, 29.

35. John Galbraith, *The Great Crash* (Boston: Houghton Mifflin, 1961); a fascinating account of 1929's "Black Tuesday" and the early days of the Great Depression.

36. James R. Adams, "Supply-Side Roots of the Founding Fathers," *Wall Street Journal* (Nov. 17, 1981), p. 26.

37. Henry Clay Lindgren, *Great Expectations, the Psychology of Money* (Los Altos, CA: William Kaufmann, 1980), p. 19.

38. Walter W. Haines, *Money, Prices and Policy* (New York: McGraw-Hill, 1958), pp. 24–25.

39. Paul Hellman, *Wall Street Journal* (Jan. 31, 1990), editorial page.

40. Quoted from *The Arizona Republic* (Jan. 4, 1986), p. 1E.

41. "Angry Workers Desecrate Flag in Milwaukee," *St. Paul Pioneer Press* (Nov. 20, 1981), p. 1.

42. Arthur Schlesinger, Jr., *Wall Street Journal* (Dec. 22, 1989), editorial page.

43. William J. Baumol, "U.S. Industry's Lead Gets Bigger." *Wall Street Journal* (March 21, 1990).

44. Herbert Stein, "Who's Number One? Who Cares?" *Wall Street Journal* (March 1, 1990), editorial page.

45. Frances Moore Lappe, *Diet for a Small Planet* (New York: Ballantine Books, 1975).

46. It should be noted that a growing number of economists are concerned that the less developed countries are adopting large-

scale technology. This is happening because they want to emulate developed countries' production techniques, and because middle or "intermediate" technology is simply not available. One economist who not only described the problem but also started "intermediate technology groups" to develop tools and equipment more suited for poor, labor intensive countries is the late E. F. Schumacher. See E. F. Schumacher, *Small Is Beautiful,* (New York: Harper & Row, 1975) and the follow-up book by George McRobie, *Small Is Possible* (New York: Harper & Row, 1981).

47. Mortz Thomsen, *Living Poor: A Peace Corps Chronicle* (Seattle: University of Washington Press, 1969).

48. Pranay Gupta, *The Crowded Earth* (New York: Norton, 1984), p. 109.

49. Op. cit. (Thomsen), p. 173.

50. For an innovative analysis on the importance of cities and the process of import substitution, see Jane Jacob's book, *Cities and the Wealth of Nations* (New York: Random House, 1984).

51. Bill McKibben, *The End of Nature* (New York: Random House, 1989), p. 18.

52. *Economic Report of the President* (1990), p. 221.

53. Peter Raven, "One-Fifth of Earth's Species Face Extinction," *U.S.A. Today* (June 6, 1986), p. 5.

54. James Lovelock, "Only Man's Presence Can Save Nature," *Harper's Magazine* (April, 1990), p. 47.

55. Rushworth M. Kidder, "Let's Not Wait for 'Proof' on Warning of Global Warming," *The Christian Science Monitor* (June 27, 1988).

56. Janet Raloff, "CO_2: How Will We Spell Relief?" *Science News* (Dec. 24, 31, 1988). For example, the utility Applied Energy Services of Arlington, VA, is helping to finance the planting of 50 million trees in Guatemala (p. 133).

57. Janet Raloff, "Governments Warm to Greenhouse Action," *Science News* (Dec. 16, 1989), p. 394.

58. Lao Tzu, *The Way of Life,* trans. by Witter Bynner (New York: Capricorn Books, 1944), p. 65.

Index

Bold page numbers refer to key terms and concepts presented in the text.